The Leadership Clock: Your Time to Lead Is Now!

MASTERS OF THE MENTAL GAME SERIES BOOK

This book is being given to

_____

Because I care about you and your success

_____

Brian M. Cain, MS, CMAA
with Brett Basham

Brian Cain Peak Performance, LLC

WHAT CHAMPIONS ARE SAYING ABOUT BRIAN CAIN, BRETT BASHAM & *THE LEADERSHIP CLOCK*

"Absolutely fantastic! Really took the complex world of leadership and made it simple and coachable."

Kevin Ozee
Athletic Director
Southlake Carroll High School, TX

"*The Leadership Clock* gives you the tools you need to succeed as a leader in college athletics. His program is straightforward and intense. He held my attention for over four hours. It was life changing."

Ben Orloff
University of California, Irvine
All-American Baseball Player

"This program is not only for sports performance... this is a pathway for life success. I am a better coach because I attended this session. Brian Cain & Brett Basham are the real deal. Every university athletic program should offer their training for student athletes and coaches on *The Leadership Clock.*"

Tim Esmay
Head Baseball Coach
Arizona State University

"This was the most beneficial presentation our school has put on in my four years here. I just wish they had Cain and Bash here my freshman year. I would have been a much better leader."

Chantal Morse
NCAA Student Athlete

"Cain gives you easy-to-use strategies that will help your students take their leadership to the next level."

Mike O'Day
Athletic Director
South Burlington High School, VT

"One of the most engaging and informative books on leadership I have ever read. This is a game changer for coaches and captains to get on the same page and lead their team the right way."

Garrett Black
Athletic Director
Greenbrier High School, GA

"Cain gives your coaches and athletes everything he has, every time out. I have worked with him for the last ten years and he truly lives his messages in *The Leadership Clock*."

Brandi Rideout
Senior Women's Administrator
Upper Iowa University

"What Cain does is a tremendous use of intensity, humor, magic and story to keep his audience engaged in the learning process. He has a gift to teach and change lives through leadership. I saw this happen right before my eyes. Our coaches and athletes raved about his *Leadership Clock* seminar."

Eric Davis
Athletic Director
Hanford High School, WA

"Brian Cain & Brett Basham's *Leadership Clock for Coaches* is one of the greatest events we have ever provided for our coaches and athletes. If you are looking for a program that will change lives and give your coaches the leadership strategies for success both on and off the field, look no further. You have that program in your hands."

Philip O'Neal
Executive Director of Athletics
Weatherford High School
Fort Bend ISD, Texas

"I've been coaching for over 25 years and have attended many student athlete development and educational seminars at all of the places I have coached. I have never taken so many notes or been more inspired to coach than I am now after this seminar."

George Horton
Head Baseball Coach
University of Oregon

MASTERS OF THE MENTAL GAME SERIES BOOK

The Leadership Clock: Your Time to Lead Is Now!

MASTERS OF THE MENTAL GAME SERIES BOOK

Brian M. Cain, MS, CMAA
with Brett Basham

Brian Cain Peak Performance, LLC

Brian M. Cain, MS, CMAA
Peak Performance Coach
Peak Performance Publishing
Brian Cain Peak Performance, LLC

The Leadership Clock: Your Time to Lead Is Now!

A Masters of the Mental Game Series Book
©2013 by Brian M. Cain, MS, CMAA, with Brett Basham

Printed in the United States of America
Edited by: Brett Basham & Mary Lou Schueler
Cover design & book layout: Brett Basham
Illustrations: Brett Basham
Photography: Various Artists

Brian M. Cain, MS, CMAA, with Brett Basham

*The Leadership Clock:
Your Time to Lead Is Now!*

A Masters of the Mental Game Series Book
Brian M. Cain, MS, CMAA
p. cm.

ISBN-13: 978-1497322417

ISBN-10: 1497322413

CONTENTS

DEDICATION 15

ACKNOWLEDGMENTS.......................17

PREFACE 19

INTRODUCTION
ARE YOU A LEADER OR A MANAGER?
Characteristics That Separate Leaders
    and Managers 25

PART I: Learning Who You Are 29

1:00 - Core Values and Vision:
What They Look Like in Action....................31
    Developing Core Values..................... 32
    5 Steps to Creating Core Values......... 33
    Having a Vision................................ 36
    Don't Confuse Vision with a Mission
        Statement 39
    4 Vision Levels of People................... 39
    1:00 Summary................................. 41
    1:00 Application............................... 41

2:00 – Character:
Who Are You? 43
    Focus on Character, not Reputation ... 45
    Character Revealed........................... 47
    Loyalty... 48
    Honesty 50
    Toughness 52
    The Law of the Palm Tree 53

The Man in the Glass........................54
2:00 Summary...............................56
2:00 Application............................57

3:00 - Self-Discipline:
A Lifestyle, not an Event......................59
How to Develop Self-Discipline...........59
Routines.....................................61
Spending Time vs. Investing Time 63
10 Tips for Better Time Prioritization ..65
Control What You Can Control 67
Story of a Traveling Man 68
Four Levels of Change......................68
Two Pains in Life............................69
Adaptability 70
The Competitor..............................71
Plan Your Day the Night Before..........73
3:00 Summary...............................76
3:00 Application............................76

PART II: Working on Yourself 77

4:00 - Accountability:
Accepting Responsibility 79
Transfer of Blame 80
Accept Responsibility.......................83
Entitlement..................................84
Three Rules of Response-Ability 85
The Problem Is not the Problem.........86
Stop Complaining,
    "Compared to What"....................87
The Power of "No" 89
DWYSYWD 90
4:00 Summary...............................93

4:00 Application.............................. 94

5:00 - Positive Energy:
Attitude Is Contagious...................... 95
    Attitude.. 99
    Eagles vs. Ducks............................ 100
    Fountains vs. Drains....................... 100
    Feed the Positive Dog 101
    Overcoming Adversity 102
    Adversity Is to Be Embraced............. 103
    Failure as Fuel 104
    8 Reasons to Embrace Failure........... 105
    Have to vs. Get to.......................... 106
    Compared to What? 107
    YET = Delayed Success................... 108
    Perseverance................................. 110
    5:00 Summary............................... 112
    5:00 Application............................. 113

6:00 - Emotional Control:
Emotion Clouds Reality..................... 115
    Sports Is not Life or Death 116
    The Inverted U of Self-Control.......... 118
    Pool Shark Analogy 118
    Golf Analogy................................. 119
    4 Ways People Deal with Emotion...... 120
    Act Differently than How You Feel 121
    Acting – Feeling – Thinking 122
    Perception Is Reality 122
    EQ 123
    Think Before You Speak
        (or Press Send) 125
    6:00 Summary............................... 128
    6:00 Application............................. 129

<u>PART III: Learning to Lead</u>..........131

7:00 - Lead Verbally and by Example:
Communication Is Key..................................133
    Must Lead Verbally and with Words....135
    Psychology & Physiology Connection..135
    Communication..................................136
    Three Standards to Lead Your Team ..
    The Power of Why 137
    Modeling Leadership 138
    Pyramid of Leadership.......................139
    7:00 Summary..................................141
    7:00 Application................................142

8:00 - Focus on the Process:
Destination Is the Disease,
Journey Is the Reward 143
    The Law of Averages........................145
    Focus on Process, not Outcome 145
    Run Your Marathon 147
    Patience in the Process......................147
    The Penalty of Youth........................147
    What Is vs. What If..........................148
    In vs. Into 149
    W.I.N. – What's Important Now........152
    Sum of "Todays"..............................153
    Don't Count the Days 153
    Release Your Mental Bricks...............154
    8:00 Summary..................................156
    8:00 Application................................157

9:00 - Pursuit of Excellence:
You vs. Yesterday 159
    Picking up Pennies 159

Focus on Being Best Version of You ... 160
10 Traits of the Best of the Best 161
The Problem with Average 162
Decision Shapes Destiny................... 163
When Have You Succeeded? 163
Success Leaves Clues....................... 164
Study the Best................................ 165
Perfection Is Unattainable 166
The Quest for Perfection 166
F.E.A.R. –
    False Evidence Appearing Real 167
Two Fears in Life 167
Perfection Is a Double-edged Sword .. 168
Kaizen.. 169
Expensive vs.
    Inexpensive Experience 170
Attention to Detail........................... 171
Performance Excellence 173
3 Steps
    for Performance Improvement...... 173
9:00 Summary................................. 177
9:00 Application.............................. 178

<u>PART IV: Making the People Around</u>
<u>You Better</u>... 179

10:00 - Confidence:
A Choice and Action, not a Feeling............... 181
    Confidence Is Critical 182
    Feelings Are False............................. 182
    ABC's of Confidence 183
    Feeding the Two Wolves 183
    Leaders Make Decisions 184
    Knowing vs. Finding out What to Do .. 185

Humility..186
3 Keys to Confidence........................187
Advertise to Yourself 188
The 10 Deadly Words.......................189
Belief –
    the Gift that Keeps on Giving........192
Preparation.....................................194
Poise..194
10:00 Summary 197
10:00 Application 198

11:00 - Ability to Inspire and Motivate:
Look Inside of You and See What You Find ..199
    "68" 200
Take the Air Out 201
    4 Factors of Motivation....................202
    Take a Look Inside,
        See What You Find 203
    You + Motivation = Success 206
    FedEx Logo Changes Lives................207
    Commitment.................................208
    Goal Setting.................................209
    Smart Goals.................................209
    3 Steps for Goal Attainment.............210
    Vision Boards................................211
    Thermostat or Thermometer.............212
    11:00 Summary 216
    11:00 Application 217

12:00 - Selflessness:
It is about WE, not ME 219
    Making the Call 220
    It's about We, not Me.......................222
    Check Your Ego at the Door..............223

Once You Master You,
    It's not about You......................224
Learn to Listen 226
Leaders Listen 227
Active Listening 228
Talk with vs. Talk to.........................229
Role Acceptance vs. Role Execution ...229
Selfless Leadership:
    Teammate Assessment 230
12:00 Summary 234
12:00 Application 234

**ABOUT THE AUTHOR
WHO IS BRIAN M. CAIN?** 235

WHO IS BRETT K. BASHAM? 237

ADDITIONAL RESOURCES...................239

CONNECT WITH CAIN 241

CONCENTRATION GRIDS 243

NOTES PAGES 247

DEDICATION

This book is dedicated to those who have made leadership a lifestyle and not an event.

To the leaders that understand people need a motto to say and more importantly a model to see, and that have been the model for others to see.

To the amazing people we have met and will meet along the journey into teaching the strategies for success in *The Leadership Clock.*

Brett Basham dedicates this book to my wife, Mary Margaret, who inspires and holds me accountable every day. To my parents, Bruce and Donna, who showed me what it was like to be selfless and put others before yourself. To my sister, Brittney, who inspires me with positive energy every day.

Brian Cain dedicates this book to Brett Basham, a selfless man with impeccable integrity and a passion for teaching leadership to leaders so they can be the most effective and empowering leaders they can be. Bash, I will never forget our time coaching together in the summer of 2013. We talked about life, and when I expressed that I wanted more, your leadership advice changed my life. You said, "Cainer, if you want more, you must become more." Thank you for your words, and thank you for inspiring me and leading me down the path of writing this book. You are the future of leadership education, my friend. Go change the world, one leader at a time.

ACKNOWLEDGMENTS

It is with sincere and deep appreciation that we acknowledge the support and guidance of the following people who helped make this project possible.

Mike Bianco, Carl Lafferty, Cliff Godwin, Jim Schlossnagle, Tim Esmay, Jeff Willis, Brian Owens, Erin Wente, Dr. Ken Ravizza, Dr. Robert Gilbert, Bruce Brown, Dan Nolan, Eric Davis, Mary Schuler and the countless others who have helped craft our vision of *The Leadership Clock: Your Time to Lead Is Now!*

PREFACE

What is Leadership? It is influence. Leaders are mirrors for the entire team to see the example of what should be done and what should not be tolerated. You serve as the benchmark for everyone else, setting the standard for those you lead.

Remove for a moment the moral issues behind it, and in its simplest form leadership is the ability to obtain followers. I'm sure you would agree with me that followers are crucial to becoming a leader. Without followers, you are simply taking a walk. Leadership is about followers, yes, and it is also about what you do with and how you get those followers to be the best they can be. The best compliment a leader can receive is not that they had a great number of followers, but that they were able to create those great followers into fellow great leaders.

Many people think leadership is holding a certain position or title such as captain, coach or CEO. Therefore, they go after that rank, position or title. When they achieve that position, they think they have become a leader. This creates two problems:

1. Those who possess the "status" of leader often experience the frustration of few people willing to follow them.

2. Those who do not possess a traditional leadership "title" may not see themselves as leaders and do not develop their leadership skills.

Oftentimes we see ordinary people with extraordinary determinations go on to become great leaders. That is because leadership is a skill that must be developed and followers must be earned - they are not granted or given.

Leadership is earned; it is not given nor are you born with it. Your birth certificate does not say, "you are a leader." Some may be born into a family that has strong parents with certain leadership qualities, but true leadership is a process that is developed over time, and it can be developed by anyone who is willing to work at the skill of leadership.

Leadership is a challenge. You will face many obstacles, adversities and setbacks. The penalty of leadership is that people will not always agree with or like your decisions. Even though decisions are in the best interest of the team, they may not be in its individuals' best interest.

In the end, they will always respect you, which is more important. Remember, the man who wants to lead the orchestra must turn his back to the crowd.

You must learn how to inspire people to achieve excellence, which is being at their best when it means the most, every day.

Responsibilities of leadership can be described as being "all in, all the time." You must be aware of the past, deeply focused on and connected with the present, and constantly scanning the horizon for what the future will bring.

Leadership is taking charge and exceeding expectations. You cannot consistently produce on a level higher than your leadership and character allow you to. In other words, your leadership skills determine the level of your success, and the success of those around you.

In life you are either growing or dying, never staying the same. Change is inevitable. The world is always evolving and always changing. Growth is optional. Leaders make the conscious choice to always be growing, or they start to die.

Leaders are always the best learners. They know they must learn as if they were to live forever, and live as if they were to die tomorrow. They know that they are students first, before anything else. We must learn to lead ourselves before we can ever lead others. Before we can exceed the expectations of others, we must first raise expectations for ourselves. We must lead for the benefit of others and not for the enrichment of ourselves.

Respect

How is great leadership developed? Through the mastering of twelve characteristics:

1. Established core values and vision

2. Impeccable character and integrity

3. Disciplined daily habits and actions

4. Public and self-accountability

5. A positive energy and attitude

6. Self-control of your mental, emotional and physical self

7. The ability to lead both verbally and by example

8. Trust in their process

9. Commitment to excellence

10. Contagious confidence in themselves and others

11. The ability to inspire and motivate others

12. Selfless service to others

To YOU, the coach, athlete, parent, student and/or corporate warrior who wants to take your leadership skills to the next level: The clock you are about to learn is serious business. Leadership should not be taken lightly. Your clock is ticking, and the time to lead is now!

Brian M. Cain, MS, CMAA
Leadership & Mental Conditioning Expert

Brett Basham
Leadership Development Consultant

> *If you are interested in bringing our Leadership Clock: Your Time to Lead Is Now workshop to your area, please visit www.briancain.com and fill out our Contact page.*

INTRODUCTION

ARE YOU A LEADER OR A MANAGER?

Characteristics that Separate Leaders and Managers

We have often heard the terms *leadership* and *management* used interchangeably. The general consensus was that "they are one and the same." However, they are very different. Most people now recognize that there is a significant difference between the two.

Management is at its best when things stay the same. Sports fans often hear the term in a negative light when used to characterize a quarterback in football: "game manager." Managers make sure that everyone is doing their job and keeping the status quo.

Leadership deals with people and their dynamics, which are continually changing. Leadership is taking a situation and inspiring followers to be better than they thought they could be.

In a 1997 ad campaign by Apple Inc. called "The Crazy Ones," it was stated: "The people who are crazy enough to think they can change the world are the ones that usually do." That thinking is what sets apart leaders from managers.

Our experience in the field of leadership development shows that there are some fundamental characteristics that set leaders apart from managers:

1. Managers are about stability and maintenance, while leaders are all about growth and change.

2. Managers make the rules, while leaders adapt and adjust for the sake of the team.

3. Managers plan details, while leaders set the direction of where the team is going.

4. Managers execute the culture, while leaders create and shape the culture.

5. Managers try to avoid conflict, while leaders use conflict as an asset because they understand that there is no progress without friction.

6. Managers use the existing roads where things are comfortable, while leaders create new roads and become comfortable with being uncomfortable.

7. Managers tend to take credit, while leaders are selfless and give the credit to the team for helping them succeed.

8. Managers make the decisions, while leaders support decisions by encouraging and listening to everyone's voice.

9. Managers tell, and leaders sell. They sell the vision and direction they are going with enthusiasm because

they know the last four letters of enthusiasm stand for I am sold myself.

10. Managers are transactional; what are the transactions to get something from someone? A leaders is transformational, transforming the team members that he/she leads into becoming more.

11. Management is doing things right. Leadership is doing the right things.

12. Managers manage people and things. Leaders develop followers by being the example others want to emulate.

The problem with management is that people do not respond well to being managed and told what to do as they once did. Micromanaging is not a leadership style; it's more of a leadership failure. People do not want to be managed. They want to be led. They want their leaders to treat them like they are part of a team and allow them to feel as if they have a part ownership of the process.

Here is a great self-assessment to see whether you are leading or managing:

> *If my position, title, role or formal authority were removed, will the people that I'm leading still gladly follow me? If you cannot answer that question honestly, ask those around you and ask them to give you a truthful answer.*

When it all comes down to it, people don't want to be managed; rather, they want to be led. They want to follow a leader.

In this book we will train you to execute some of the fundamental leadership skills we have experienced in the greatest leaders we have worked with.

PART I

LEARNING WHO YOU ARE

1:00

CORE VALUES & VISION:

What They Look Like in Action

What is your WHY?

Why is it that you do what you do?

These two questions are the key to developing core values. Core values are personal beliefs and qualities reinforced through a commitment to yourself and your teammates. Your values are the "compass" that is guiding you and your team to its ultimate destiny.

Anytime you have difficulty making an important decision, you can be sure that it's the result of being unclear about your values. Values are fundamental principles that should be integrated into the routines of your daily life. They will provide an internal guide to direct you on your journey and will reflect how you approach your pursuit of excellence. If you are not living your values regularly, you will end up forgetting why it is you do what you do.

We have all seen teams that have goals they want to achieve but no values to rely on when things get tough. Team members have their own ideas of what is important, which leads to confusion. The team cannot survive if its members do things how they want to do them. This is why values become important.
Just like values for your personal life guide your daily decisions, your team's core values influence the direction of the team and create your culture.

If you want your team to reach its potential, you must have a firm set of core values and be able to live them on and off the field.

DEVELOPING CORE VALUES

You must identify your personal and team core values in order to realize what you stand for, both now and in the future. Please reflect upon the following question:

How do you want to be remembered when your last journey is over?

_____

_____

_____

At the celebration of your life, what do you want people to say about you as a person who was committed to leading others on the pursuit of excellence?

_____

_____

_____

Answering these questions will help provide clarity to what is most significant to you and how you will want to begin leading yourself and others.

As you keep reflecting, consider how your core values transfer to your sport. Think about how you would like people to acknowledge you and your contributions to that sport and your team.

5 STEPS TO CREATING CORE VALUES

1. Who am I? Who are we? The first step is to identify who we need to become as a person or as a team.

2. How would I define who I need to become or who we need to become as a team?

Value #1 _____

Definition _____

Value #2 _____

Definition _____

Value #3 _____

Definition _____

Value #4 _____

Definition _____

Value #5 _____

Definition _____

3. Describe what that looks like in 4 key areas:
School/Education/Growth/Training

_____

_____

Social/Community

_____

_____

Athletics/Career

_____

_____

Personal Life

_____

_____

4. Self-assess the current status of how each player and we as a team are living these core values.

5. Create personal development plans with an accountability partner and accountability structure (daily, weekly).

Your focus should be anywhere between three to five core values. Our experience shows that more than five is possible, yet with most high-level achievers, less is more.

Giving yourself a more narrowed focus will increase your chances for a successful mastery of a particular core value. Once these values are created, they must be communicated consistently and constantly. If not, your core values become like most organizations' mission statements - a paragraph on a wall that nobody knows or can describe, let alone use to guide their daily decisions.

We must be clear about what is most important in our lives and decide that we will live by these values, no matter what happens. This consistency must occur regardless of whether the environment rewards us for living by our standards or not. We must live by our values even when it rains on our parade.

The most consistent way for us to have long-term success is to live by our highest standards, to consistently agree with what we believe our life is truly about. We cannot do this if we don't know what our values are!

The biggest tragedy in life is that many people know what they want to have but have no idea of who they must become to get what they want.

Leadership trainer and speaker Jim Rohn said it best: "If you want more, you must become more." A clear set of values gives you the best chance to become all that you are capable of becoming.

HAVING A VISION

> *"Vision has no boundaries and knows no limits. Our vision is what we become in life."*
>
> **Tony Dungy, Super Bowl Winning Coach**

There was not a more captivating coach in all of sports than the late Jim Valvano. Valvano, former basketball coach at North Carolina State University and winner of the 1983 NCAA National Championship, was as outspoken and charismatic as any coach in recent history. However, he was best known for his battle with cancer, which ultimately took his life. His famous "Don't give up, don't ever give up" speech at the 1993 ESPY Awards, about his battle with cancer, is still one of the most inspirational speeches you will find.

Valvano also had a clear vision for himself and his team. At the beginning of the 1983 season, he put his team through one practice where all they did was practice cutting down the nets, customary of the team who wins the NCAA Championship. There were no basketballs out and no drills being run. The entire roster practiced cutting down the nets like teams do after a championship.

This was an event that Coach Valvano had every one of his squads do over the years. This alone was something that gave his team confidence and the belief that they were capable of winning it all. By beginning the basketball season with the end result in mind, Valvano gave his team a clear vision of where they were going. Every opportunity on the court from that day forward was a chance to live that vision.

The mindset continued throughout the year, as Valvano kept reminding his team that they would win a championship. His motivation was beyond anything that other coaches have shown in the past.

Many great leaders insist leadership starts with having a vision. First and foremost, this means clearly setting the team's direction and purpose. A vision to a leader is to take people places they never thought they would go, help them see things they normally wouldn't see, and do things they normally wouldn't do. You must lead people from where they are to where they want to go and where they ought to be. A vision is a statement about what your team is committed to becoming.

It should resonate with all members of the team and help them feel inspired and motivated to be part of something much bigger than the individual. A vision should stretch the team's capabilities and self-image. A vision gives shape and direction to the organization's future. It survives even the toughest of times and through the difficulties of adversity. If your vision changes when adversity strikes, it's not really a vision. It is more like just a dream.

A vision must be communicated, shared, and understood by all team members if the organization is to succeed. More than a goal that everyone can get behind, a great vision is a picture of success that people can share, shape and contribute to. Most people want to feel like they're working toward something real and important, not just working their way through tasks.

However, it is difficult to convince people of where you want to go when you have not FULLY convinced yourself. You must begin anything with the end in mind to give your journey a sense of purpose. You must know precisely where you want to end up and, most importantly, why you want to end up there.

All great leaders have a vision of what they want to accomplish. That vision becomes the energy behind every effort and the force that pushes through all the problems. With vision, the leader is on a mission and a contagious spirit is felt among the crowd until others begin to rise alongside the leader. Unity is essential for the dream to be realized.

Long hours of labor are gladly invested to accomplish the goal. Individual rights are set aside because the whole is much more important than the part.

Helen Keller was asked, "What would be worse than being born blind?" She replied, "To have sight without vision."

Sadly, too many people are placed into leadership positions without a vision for the team that they lead. If you don't change the direction you are going, then you're likely to end up where you're heading. A great leader's courage to fulfill his or her vision comes from passion, not position.

DON'T CONFUSE VISION WITH A MISSION STATEMENT

We've all seen mission statements that are long, full of big words and fancy slogans, and make everyone feel good. Some teams like to claim they're changing the world, thanks to revolutionary systems and perfect integrity. What they often don't realize is that attempts at being ambitious and inspirational come off as interchangeable and irrelevant. Don't confuse your vision with a mission statement. Instead of something that sounds nice, create an image of your organization's purpose, one that everyone on the team can own, contribute to and participate in. People need a model to see more than a motto to say. By having a vision, your team members know exactly what they are working towards and can see that destination vividly.

People don't want to come to work if they don't know what they're working towards, or if they can sense that their leaders don't know either. Team members have a hard time developing trust in their leader if they're unsure where the team is headed. If your team can no longer express its vision in a simple, convincing way, then you as a leader have gone off the track. Don't tell the world your mission statement. Show the world you are on a mission.

4 VISION LEVELS OF PEOPLE

You can seize only what you can see. Vision is everything for a leader. It leads the leader, displays a target, ignites the fire within, and serves as a spark plug for others who follow that leader.

We have been asked, "Does the vision make the leader, or does the leader make the vision?" Vision must always come first. At the highest level, people on your team will buy into the vision before they buy into the leader.

Here are the four vision levels of people:

1. Some people never see it. They are wanderers.

2. Some people see it but never pursue it on their own. They are followers.

3. Some people see it and pursue it. They are achievers.

4. Some people see it, pursue it, and help others see it and pursue it. They are leaders. To do the impossible, you have to see the invisible!

A great example of vision is a story about Walt Disney, the founder of Walt Disney World and Disneyland. When Disney World first opened, Mrs. Walt Disney was asked to speak at the Grand Opening, since Walt had passed away. She was introduced by a man who said, "Mrs. Disney, I just wish Walt could have seen this." She stood up and said, "He did," and sat down.

Walt Disney knew it. He had a vision from the beginning, and now people all over the world get to experience that vision.

1:00 SUMMARY

The key to developing core values is answering these questions: What is your WHY? Why is it that you do what you do?

How do you want to be remembered when your last journey is over?

You must begin with the end in mind.

To do the impossible, you have to see the invisible.

You must lead people from where they are to where they want to go and where they ought to be.

Don't confuse vision with a mission statement.

1:00 APPLICATION

What are 5 key points you can apply to yourself and your team from this chapter?

1) _____

2) _____

3) _____

4) _____

5) _____

2:00

CHARACTER:
Who Are You?

> *"The softest pillow is a clear conscience."*
>
> **John Wooden**
> **Former UCLA Basketball Coach**

As a leader, the people you lead count on you to do the right thing no matter what the situation entails. They will expect you to know right from wrong, to act accordingly, and hold yourself accountable to a higher standard. What you have to realize is that many are watching what you do. You must understand that all of your actions either reflect positively or negatively on the rest of the team.

Nick Saban, head football coach at The University of Alabama, had this to say about character:

> *Character is an accumulation of your thoughts, habits, and priorities. In other words, what you think, what you do, and what's important to you. Those things determine the choices that you make. The choices that you make determine who you are.*

Character is a choice. It is what you do when no one is watching. Most people slack off or take the easy road when no one is looking or when they think their lack of effort will go undetected. Someone is always watching. It's doing the right thing all the time, even when it may work to your disadvantage. It is the internal compass and rudder that directs you to where you know you should go when everything around you is pulling in a different direction. Do what you say you will do, no matter the circumstances.

John Maxwell, famed leadership expert, had this to say about character:

> *A person with character does not have divided loyalties; that is duplicity. They also do not pretend; that is hypocrisy. Character is not what we do so much as who we are. Who we are determines what we do. Our core values are so much a part of us we cannot separate it from ourselves. It becomes the navigating system that guides us. It establishes priorities in our lives and judges what we will accept or reject.*

The core values you set for your life will determine your attitude and your altitude. Your core values serve as your internal GPS that re-routes you when you make a wrong turn or have a question about where you are going or where you are on your journey.

FOCUS ON CHARACTER, NOT REPUTATION

Legendary UCLA basketball coach John Wooden said:

> *Be more concerned with your character than your reputation, because your character is what you really are, while your reputation is merely what others think you are.*

Basketball enthusiasts can quote John Wooden's winning basketball statistics and leaders around the world can quote his character-centered leadership principles. While people are impressed with Wooden's 10 NCAA championships in 12 years and his 88 consecutive wins, it is the coach's unwavering commitment to building character, demonstrating integrity, and focusing on values that most impressed those who worked with him and those who admired his work from afar.

Here are five characteristics showing why character is more important than reputation:

1. Character builds trust: Trust is the force that connects people to the leader and their vision.   If my teammates understand me, I'll get their attention.   If my teammates trust me, I'll inspire them to act.   The moment trust is lost, a leader's power to influence is lost as well.

You can't have a strong team without strong relationships.   And you can't have strong relationships without trust.   Great leaders trust their teammates and, most of all, their team members trust them.   Trust is earned through integrity, consistency, honesty, transparency, vulnerability and dependability.   If you can't be trusted, you can't be a great team member. Trust is everything.

2. Character means leading myself before leading others.   We cannot lead anyone else farther than we have been ourselves. Too many times people are more focused on the destination and try to shortcut the process.   There are no shortcuts when character is involved.   Destination is the disease; journey is the reward.

3. Character helps a leader be dependable.   Leaders who are sincere don't have to advertise the fact.   It's noticeable in their daily habits and soon becomes evident to the rest of the team.

4. Character is a hard-earned achievement. "When wealth is lost, nothing is lost. When health is lost, something is lost. When character is lost, everything is lost." – Evangelist Billy Graham

5. Character results in a solid reputation, not just an image. Your answers to the following questions will determine if you are into image building instead of character building:

Are you consistent? Are you the same person no matter who you are with?

Do you put WE before ME? Do you make decisions that are best for the team when another choice would benefit you as an individual?

Do you give credit to teammates when the team succeeds and take the blame when the team fails? Do you recognize others first for their efforts and contributions to your success and the team's success?

> *"Watch your thoughts, for they become words. Watch your words, for they become actions. Watch your actions, for they become habits. Watch your habits, for they become character. Watch your character, for it becomes your destiny."*
>
> ***Chinese philosopher Lao-Tze***

CHARACTER REVEALED

Imagine you have a bottle filled with liquid. It can be any liquid: water, soft drink, or Gatorade. You are the bottle. The amount of liquid in the bottle is your character. Now, imagine if that bottle was tipped or knocked over; what would happen? Obviously, the liquid, whatever it is, would spill out.

This is what happens when adversity hits. As with the bottle in this story, when you are tipped over, the contents of your bottle will spill out. That is ultimately who you are. This is your character being revealed.

In your sport and your life, adversity will come. Your character will be tested, revealed, and further developed by the decisions you make in the most challenging times. That is how character is developed – by facing decisions and choosing the right way over and over until it becomes second nature. You will be tipped over. It is inevitable. Leaders will get back up, knowing that once the contents of the bottle are placed back in the bottle, they have grown stronger.

Coaches will try to keep tipping the bottle over and bringing it back. When you keep getting tipped over, remember one thing. Adversity does not build character; it reveals it!

LOYALTY

A quality that leaders possess and should look for in others is loyalty. This alone does not make another person successful, but a lack of loyalty is sure to kill rapport with that person. Loyalty is the foundational quality that gets us through hard times. Will you compromise your character when temptation is great?

Or will you remain loyal to your core values, teammates and coaches? You may become great in the eyes of others, but you'll never become successful when you compromise your character and show disloyalty toward coaches or teammates. The reverse is true as well: No individual or team will become great without loyalty. Your loyalty should not be available to the highest bidder.

If you are a coach or player and are looking for potential leaders, they must be loyal. If you are pondering someone who isn't loyal, that person should be dismissed if they can be replaced, or trained before they are given more responsibility.

A person cannot be a leader or an effective part of the team if they cannot be trusted or loyal.

What does it mean for a leader to be loyal, or for a person to be loyal to their leader?

1. It is to care for your people no matter what their strengths or weaknesses are. You genuinely care for each other, not just for what you can do for each other. As a coach, to be loyal to your team you need to care more about them as people than as performers in their sport.

2. Loyal people always represent you well to others. They have nothing but positive things to say about you, and when given the opportunity to defame you, they choose to remain silent or choose the road to build you up. They may hold you accountable, but never condemn.

HONESTY

Honesty is a critically important character trait of a leader. Honesty is doing what we know is right. Honesty is not giving in to the temptation to do something that may help us in the moment but what we know is wrong.

Honesty must occur at all times, in both thought and action. Honest people stay the course, regardless of the consequences. If we are honest, our character will not allow us to compromise.

Being dishonest is often an attempt to deceive someone. It is possible to be so deceptive that we deceive ourselves. We do this when we attempt to justify a lie because of circumstances or as payback when someone has been dishonest with us.

Dishonesty, no matter the reason, destroys our credibility and costs us our self-respect. Being tempted to be dishonest is not the problem. We all face that. The lesson to learn is how to resist the temptation when it comes.

You must be willing to tell the truth when others ask for it or need to hear it, rather than avoiding the situation because it may put you in an uncomfortable position. Leaders must be brutally honest. It is the only way to keep the communication process as clean and clear as possible. Be so honest that it can shake you to your core. Honesty is necessary in helping people develop, both in their sport and in life.

The people you lead may not always like to hear the truth, but they will respect you for being truthful. You wrong the people you lead if you aren't willing to tell the truth.

You must also be honest with yourself. It is the key for any leader to be able to self-evaluate his/her strengths and weaknesses. Leaders always want the best coach to coach them. The best coach you will ever have, of course, is yourself. You must look yourself in the mirror and ask yourself if you are giving the best possible effort and trying to become all you are capable of becoming, both on the playing field and as a leader. To be the best leader you can possibly be, you have to evaluate yourself. Remember, you must learn to lead yourself before you can lead others. That starts with being honest.

 **COACHING POINT: Think back to an incident in which you stood for what was right or truthful, but there was a cost you had to pay. How did that help shape your character?**

_____

_____

_____

_____

TOUGHNESS

If you looked up toughness in the dictionary, it would be defined as being able to withstand great force without tearing or breaking; something that is strong and resilient. Toughness isn't always physical. It has nothing to do with size, physical strength or athleticism. It's an intangible, a controllable, an attitude and a philosophy. I believe true toughness is a skill that can be developed and improved in everyone.

ESPN college basketball analyst Jay Bilas writes in his book *Toughness* about toughness in many different forms. He never lists toughness as an act of physicality.

When we think of toughness, it is not always the Chuck Norrises or Rocky Balboas of the world who keep moving forward when getting hit in the mouth. That is a part of toughness. Toughness is also seen in athletes like Michael Jordan, Ray Lewis and Cal Ripken, Jr. They were characterized as tough, not for anything physical, but because they were superhuman and took tremendous punishment. It was because they were mentally unbreakable.

They were all leaders in their sport because they were able to bend while never breaking. An athlete who bends without breaking and bounces back up will prevail over the hard athlete – someone who isn't resistant to bending under pressure but will break with enough force. It is mental toughness that makes a leader unbreakable, whereas physical hardness can be more easily broken.   Tough times don't last; tough people do!

THE LAW OF THE PALM TREE

Have you ever been in a windstorm so strong that it pushes your car? The type of wind that can knock you over when you walk?   The strong wind that can do damage to the land but never do damage to the palm tree?

The palm tree knows how to bend but never break. It is indestructible.   It knows how to withstand the pressure and how to be flexible. The palm tree will be pushed and will bend, but it will never break. Oak trees will snap in half under adverse conditions like heavy winds. Not the palm tree. Like the palm tree, you must be able to bend but never break. No matter what you are faced with, you must be tough enough to handle it to lead effectively.   If you break under adverse conditions, your team will break as well.

THE MAN IN THE GLASS

In the end, you are in control of your own destiny. Your success in sports and life is most greatly influenced by you and your actions. I first heard this poem when I was in the 10th grade and it has stayed with me ever since.

What do you see when you look in the mirror?

When you get what you want in your struggle for self and the world makes you king for a day, just go to your mirror and look at yourself and see what that man has to say.

For it isn't your father or mother or wife whose judgment upon you must pass. The one whose verdict counts most in this life is the man staring back from the glass.

He's the one to please, never mind all the rest, for he's with you clear up to the end. And you've passed your most dangerous and difficult test if the man in the glass is your friend.

You may be like Jack Horner and "chisel" a plum, and think you're a wonderful guy. But the man in the glass says you're only a bum if you can't look him straight in the eye.

You may fool the whole world through the pathway of years and get pats on the back as you pass. But your final reward will be heartache and tears if you've cheated the man in the glass.

 COACHING POINT: Who are the top three people of character that you know?

1) _____

2) _____

3) _____

What makes their character stand out to you?

_____

_____

_____

2:00 SUMMARY

Character is a choice!

Focus more on character than reputation.

Adversity doesn't build character; it reveals it.

Are you consistent? Are you the same person no matter who is with you?

Character helps a leader build trust and be dependable.

Will you compromise your character when temptation is great?

The people you lead may not always like to hear the truth, but they will respect you for telling the truth.

Your loyalty should not be available to the highest bidder.

True toughness is an intangible, a controllable, an attitude and a philosophy.

2:00 APPLICATION

What are 5 key points you can apply to yourself and your team from this chapter?

1) _____

2) _____

3) _____

4) _____

5) _____

3:00

SELF-DISCIPLINE:

A Lifestyle, not an Event

Self-discipline means doing what you're supposed to be doing, when you are supposed to do it, the way it is supposed to be done. The right way, the right thing, at the right time, all the time. It is doing what you have to do when you need to do it, whether you want to or not.

Self-discipline - the only kind of discipline that lasts. It is action oriented. Those who have self-discipline don't procrastinate and don't make excuses.

If you research those who are most successful, you will find that they all possess great self-discipline and adhere to personal development programs to achieve excellence.

People often have a negative association with the word discipline. In leadership, discipline only has a positive connotation. Behavior correction is what you do when someone breaks a rule; discipline is a habit of the highest achievers. Fortunately, discipline is also a skill that can be taught and practiced.

HOW TO DEVELOP SELF-DISCIPLINE

A way in which discipline can be developed is to force action to occur that is different from your feelings. This is important because often tasks are not completed if people don't feel like doing them. This is simply laziness getting the best of you. To combat laziness, select three things in your daily life that aren't being done that should be and challenge yourself to make them a part of your daily routine. You can refer to them as daily wins.

They can be things that you may have to wake up five minutes earlier to do. Learning how to fake it until you make it and forcing yourself to act differently than how you feel will go a long way in helping you be at your best when it means the most.

Examples of daily wins that might inspire action to occur are making your bed first thing in the morning, doing household chores when your parents tell you to, working on specific skills in your sport when you feel like watching TV, studying for a test in advance and not the night before, etc. When you complete these wins for the day and force yourself to act differently than how you feel, you build the muscle of self-discipline. Remember, discipline is a lifestyle, not something you do one time!

John Wooden said:

> I believe there are individuals with ability that become All-Americans, all-stars and all-pros who do not take care of their bodies. They may even win championships, but they are not successes. Think of what they could be if they took care of themselves. There is a vast difference between better and best.

You may be better than the rest, but you are not a success until you have made the effort to become the best you can be.

Coach Wooden is saying that success is a measure of how good you are compared to how good you could be, not how good you are compared to others. The players he talks about above did not practice the self-discipline that ultimately could have made them the best players they could have been.

 **COACHING POINT: What are three daily tasks you can perform to improve your self-discipline?**

Discipline Goal 1.

_____

Discipline Goal 2.

_____

Discipline Goal 3.

_____

ROUTINES

During the week prior to Super Bowl XLVIII in MetLife Stadium between the Denver Broncos and Seattle Seahawks, I listened to a sports radio show that included an interview with former Dallas Cowboys quarterback Troy Aikman. He was discussing current Broncos quarterback Peyton Manning.

Manning is widely considered one of the greatest players in NFL history. Two things of importance from that interview shed some insight into the success of Peyton Manning. Aikman said that prior to playing in his first Super Bowl game, Manning called several quarterbacks that had previous Super Bowl experience and asked them for advice.

Manning's reputation for preparation is nothing short of legend. This story just further proves the importance of leaving no stone unturned and gives more evidence as to what makes Manning so great. As for the advice that Aikman gave Manning? He told him to make his hotel as much like home as possible because he felt the most important thing in big games was maintaining routine. "Keep things as normal as possible," Aikman said.

Routine allows you to be as consistent as you can be. Stephen Covey, author of *The Seven Habits of Highly Successful People,* said, "The main thing is to keep the main thing the main thing." Leaders are able to keep the main thing the main thing and stay focused on what they want to do that day amidst the massive amount of distraction that is guaranteed to come their way. They eliminate clutter that keeps them from accomplishing the task at hand.

Secrets of success are hidden in the routines of our daily lives. The purpose of any routine is to set the stage for consistent performance.

Routines are effective at this because they give structure by providing a consistent starting point to activate regular procedure. The familiarity of routines establishes good performance habits, and your investment in cultivating them will pay big dividends on your pursuit of excellence.

In basketball, a player shooting a free throw relies on routine for confidence and consistency at the free throw line. When golfers get away from their performance routines, they do not perform at their peak.

The effectiveness of a routine in a high-pressure situation is a result of the hard work and time put into preparation, and of the mental toughness it takes to stick to that routine when your mind wants to speed up and take you out of it.

Routines are huge timesavers when it pertains to our daily lives and let us perform at our best because we are familiar and confident in what we are doing.

SPENDING TIME VS. INVESTING TIME

In the movie *In Time*, starring Justin Timberlake, scientists unlock the secret to immortality. People are genetically modified to stop aging at 25 years old, and after that a clock is activated with one more year for each citizen. Time becomes the new currency, and one desperate man comes under attack from a mysterious group known only as the "Timekeepers," who control the society. As the threat of overpopulation looms over society, money becomes a thing of the past. Now assets are measured in time, and those with the most time also possess the most power. The old saying that time is money is very true.

We are all blessed with certain things in life, whether that is athletic ability, intelligence, etc. One thing we are not blessed with more than any other person is TIME. That's the one thing that makes everyone equal. You look at your watch, you look at my watch; you look at your clock, you look at my clock; you look at your phone, you look at my phone. It is all the same. Time slows down for no one. There is only one factor between everyone in the world who is competing for what you want: We all have only 86,400 seconds in a day. You will notice successful leaders do not disrespect their time. Most people will spend time; leaders will INVEST time. Treat time carelessly, and it will do the same to you and your team.

When you spend time, you get nothing in return; it is gone forever and you will never get it back. When you invest time, while the time is gone, you will get an enormous return in the future. If you are not efficient with your time, the competitors who are will pass you by. Learn to take control and advantage of your time, or your time will take control and advantage of you.

Time is the scarcest resource, and unless it is managed, nothing else can be managed. Your intentional use of time will offend and confuse people that desire status quo. Remember, you can earn more money, you can get more friends - but when time is gone, it is gone forever.

We often classify these concepts as time management. I believe we need to focus on time prioritization, one step before time management. One great example of time prioritization is to write what you want to accomplish the next day on your bathroom mirror with a dry erase marker. Write down your core values, positive messages, and some key goals you want to accomplish throughout the following day.

This provides an effective method of preparing for the next day. When you go to bed, you will be relaxed, knowing you already have a jump-start on the new day.

10 TIPS FOR BETTER TIME PRIORITIZATION

1. Make a list of everything you do in a day, from the time you wake up until the time you go to sleep. At the end of the day, assess all that you have accomplished and where your time could be spent more efficiently the next day.

2. Not everything has to or ever will be perfect. Realize that not every task demands your utmost concern and care. You can only do a few things at a level of excellence. Make the choice to be well rounded and do everything well or WORLD CLASS, and do a few things better than anyone in the world.

3. Take a deep breath and recognize that you too need breaks. Remember that even the President has time to vacation.

4. Clean up your home or locker that may be cluttered or unorganized. Once these spaces are clean, you will

notice how much time it will save you not having to search for something.

5. Work smarter, not harder. If you had a headache and were prescribed two Advil, you would not take twenty and expect the headache to go away 10 times faster. Many people take the approach that working longer and harder will yield quicker results. This is not always an effective way to work and live. Don't confuse activity with productivity. Working hard at the wrong things doesn't work either.

6. Figure out what time of day you are most productive. Complete tasks that need the most attention and require the most brain activity at this time.

7. Don't procrastinate. Be productive and realize that you are only putting off the pain of having to do the job in the near future. A time will come when the job needs to be done, and it will be nice to know you already completed it. Do it RIGHT NOW.

8. Avoid interruptions. They cause you to get off task and then it takes more time to get back in the present moment that you were previously working in. Refocus and get back to the present and the process.

9. Don't exhaust your time. Work as long as you are productive. When you run out of energy, you are only prolonging jobs that could be done in half the time.

10. Learn to say "No." You do not need to feel pressured into committing to things when you already know you have a full workload.

CONTROL WHAT YOU CAN CONTROL

I have worked with Jim Schlossnagle, the head baseball coach at Texas Christian University sine 2006. He teaches the controllable aspects of the game. Every time we were together as a team, he referenced attitude and energy as the only things that were in our control on the field. This allowed our team to perform at the highest level because they weren't focused on what they could not control, how many hits they had or how many people they struck out. They were focused on the name on the front of their jersey and how much energy they could bring to the field.

The results of the "control what you can control" approach paid off as we advanced to the 2010 NCAA College World Series. By being aware of our attitude and energy, we could control them.

What you are aware of you can control; what you are unaware of is going to control you.

You can also control your perspective and how you choose to look at different situations. Are you a "have to" or a "get to" leader? When faced with completing a task that may not be high on your priority list at the moment, do you say, "I have to do this" or do you say, "I get to do this"? When you choose the perspective of "I get to," you are immediately changing to a positive perspective, allowing yourself to have the best chance to improve and be successful.

STORY OF A TRAVELING MAN

A man sat on a park bench when a traveler stopped by and asked, "What are the people like in this city?" The man on the bench then asked, "What are the people like where you came from?" The traveler said, "They were a horrible bunch - mean, backstabbing and rude." The man on the bench looked the traveler in the eye and said, "You will find the same people here in this city."

About an hour later, a second traveler approached the man on the bench and asked, "What are the people like in this city?" The man on the bench then asked, "What are the people like where you came from?" The second traveler said: "They are wonderful. The nicest warm and welcoming bunch you would ever find. It is so hard to leave, but my job takes me here." The man sat up on the bench, looked the traveler in the eye and said, "You will find the same people here in this city."

What this story illustrates is that you will find what you are looking for. If you are looking for negativity, you will find it. If you are looking for positivity, it is most certainly there. Your perspective is a reflection of yourself.

FOUR LEVELS OF CHANGE

People can be resistant to change because they often think they are living the best life they can in that moment or common sense would tell them to do something else. Unfortunately, common sense is not a common practice. As a leader, you are a change artist who gets others to change their ideas or perspectives because they want to do so. Understanding the four levels of change will help you to better understand where you are on the change continuum with others.

1. Resistance to change. "That is not for me."

2. Good idea for others to try. "That is working for other people, but it's not for me."

3. Are willing to try it out themselves. "It's working for others so I will give it a shot."

4. Can't believe they lived without the change. "How did I ever live without it?"

TWO PAINS IN LIFE

Each day you must choose either the pain of discipline or the pain of regret. Discipline is a daily habit that all successful leaders abide by. It is not a one-time thing but is a lifestyle that great leaders create. They force themselves to be disciplined in the short term so they can be successful in the long term. Discipline is tough, and something you may try to avoid. But in sports and in life, short-term pain is often the only path to long-term gain. In the heat of battle it is too late to prepare. Either you are ready for the challenges of your sport and life or you will be haunted by the "what ifs," "if onlys," and "I should haves" that accompany the failure to be prepared. That's the pain of regret.

> "We must all suffer from one of two pains: the pain of discipline or the pain of regret. The difference is discipline weighs ounces while regret weighs tons."
>
> **Jim Rohn**
> **Motivational Speaker**

ADAPTABILITY

In life there are many things that we cannot be sure of, but one thing we can be sure of is change. We need to recognize change, grow with it and learn from it. Change is inevitable; people who are inflexible, stubborn and resistant to change will never reach the peak of success. If we want to succeed, we must readily adapt to circumstances as they unfold – this includes both what we cannot change and what will take some time to change.

To take advantage of changing circumstances, we must survey the situation and then make the necessary adjustments. We may need to bring in new personnel, change a routine or change our course of action. We change what we can - but if we get too concerned, too involved or too engrossed in circumstances over which we have no control or cannot change, those circumstances are going to have a negative impact on events and outcomes we can control. Great coaches will adapt their coaching style to the personnel that they have with that year's team.

THE COMPETITOR

An enemy I had, whose face I stoutly strove to know, for hard he dogged my steps unseen, wherever I did go. My plans he balked, my aims he foiled, he blocked my onward way. When for some lofty goal toiled, he grimly said to me, Nay. One night I seized him and held him fast, from him the veil did draw, I looked upon his face at last and lo... myself I saw.

COACHING POINT: List the three most disciplined people you know and why you said that about them.

1) _____

_____

2) _____

_____

3) _____

_____

What are some things disciplined leaders do in practice?

_____

_____

What are some things disciplined leaders do in games?

_____

_____

What are some things disciplined leaders do in school?

_____

_____

What are some things disciplined leaders do in their personal lives?

_____

_____

As a leader, what does discipline mean to you, and how can you demonstrate it to your team?

_____

_____

	Controllables	Uncontrollables
Community		
School		
Athletics		
Personal		

PLAN YOUR DAY THE NIGHT BEFORE

The average number of hours you are awake each day is 16. There is no reason why you can't make the most of each one. Yet, at the end of the day, many people usually end up wishing they had more time or wondering why they failed to maximize the day. This is why, to get the most out of every hour you're awake, it's important to plan your day ahead of time. More specifically, do it the night before.

To plan your day, think of some of the common, everyday things you do — the things that you would not ordinarily plan as a part of your day, like checking your e-mail, for example. The next time you're checking e-mails, watch the clock and see how much time it takes. While checking your e-mail might require 20 minutes of your time, you may end up spending 30 or more minutes dealing with the content of those messages. At the end of the day, these kinds of unexpected diversions, whether necessary or not, contribute to that sense of disappointment.

Knowing how to plan your day requires time. Because such scheduling is often overlooked or disregarded, the first step and the most effective approach is to plan to plan. Committing 30 minutes or so toward establishing a practical daily plan might seem like a waste of time, but spending the time now saves time later - and like anything, the more often you do it, the better you become. It wouldn't be unusual if you were somewhat overambitious in estimating your ability to achieve certain things at first. By doing it more and more, you get familiar with your limitations and you will get much more accomplished.

If you fail to accomplish one of the tasks you've penciled into your plan (even if it's partially or mostly finished), pencil it in for the next day. Don't cross it off and assume you'll take care of it tomorrow. For chronic list-makers there is an undeniable, if minor, sense of accomplishment in being able to cross off a task, but they only allow themselves the pleasure if it is truly completed.

3:00 SUMMARY

Self-discipline means doing what you're supposed to be doing, when you are supposed to do it, the way it is supposed to be done.

Success is a measure of how good you are compared to how good you could be, not how good you are compared to others.

Strive to accomplish three daily wins.

Secrets of success are hidden in the routines of our daily lives.

Leaders invest time, not spend it. They get a return on their investment.

Control what you can control.

Plan your day the night before.

3:00 APPLICATION

What are 5 key points you can apply to yourself and your team from this chapter?

1) _____

2) _____

3) _____

4) _____

5) _____

Part II

WORKING ON YOURSELF

4:00
ACCOUNTABILITY:
Accepting Responsibility

Dr. Earl Reum was a magician, educator and speaker. He delivered one of the best leadership seminars I have ever seen and challenges us with his wish for leaders:

> *I sincerely wish that you will have the experience of thinking up a new idea, planning it, organizing it, following it to completion, and have it be magnificently successful. I hope you'll go through the same process and have something "bomb-out."*

> *I wish you could know how it feels "to run" with all your heart and lose - horribly! I wish that you could find something so worthwhile that you deem it worthy of investigating your life within it. I hope that you become frustrated and challenged enough to begin to push back the very barriers of your own personal limitations.*

> *I hope that you make a stupid mistake and get caught red-handed and are big enough to say those magic words: "I was wrong." I hope that you give so much of*

yourself some days you wonder if it is worth the effort. I wish for you the worst kind of criticism for everything you do, because that is what makes you fight to achieve beyond what you normally would. I wish for you the experience of leadership.

Reum taught that leadership was never easy. If it were, everyone would be a leader on your team or in your school. Can you handle the responsibility that comes with leadership? Can you hold yourself and the people you lead accountable to your team's standards? That can be uncomfortable and requires toughness on both sides of the conversation, or confrontation.

But what does accountability look like? First and foremost, it means that you accept responsibility for the outcomes you achieve - both good and bad. You don't blame others, make excuses or blame the external environment. There are always things you could have done - or still can do - to change the outcome.

TRANSFER OF BLAME

If I were to ask you what America's National Pastime is, what would your answer be?
Baseball?

What if I told you that you were wrong? The real National Pastime is transfer of blame. People who have not yet learned to be leaders when it comes to accountability will find themselves blaming everyone else when things do not go well. More often than not, the blame will be directed toward sources out of their control – like the weather, the conditions of court or field, skill of the opponent, and the coach.

This type of person continues to focus on distractions, while the leader heads back to the practice floor or the weight room to work on the things that are within their control. The non-leaders consistently see themselves as victims and are seldom honest with themselves about their areas of weakness. They hesitate to tackle problems head on, preferring to sidestep any responsibility for individual or team improvement.

There are large numbers of people who fail to take responsibility for their attitudes and actions. If they're grumpy and someone asks why, they'll say, "I got up on the wrong side of the bed." When failure begins to plague their lives, they'll say, "I was born on the wrong side of the tracks." When someone else gets a promotion they wanted, it's because they were in the wrong place at the wrong time. Do you notice something? They are blaming everyone else for their problems. Instead of taking responsibility and changing their perspective, they decide to blame others. Wherever you find a problem, you will usually find the finger-pointing of blame. Every time you point a finger, there are three pointing right back at you.

Society is addicted to playing the victim card. If you change your perspective and change your attitude, you change your reality. You will never become who you want to be if you keep blaming everyone else for who you are. ***When the archer misses the target, he turns and looks for the fault within himself.***

Failure to hit the bull's-eye is never the fault of the target.

Leaders take responsibility, no matter if it's their fault or not. When things are not going well, leaders look at themselves first to see where they can make a difference. Great people, great leaders take responsibility for their mistakes, learn from them and improve from them instead of putting the blame on someone else.

To admit when you are wrong is a sign of strength, a sign of maturity and a sign of leadership. When you admit you were wrong, you show that you are logical, human and are governed by what is right, not by a need to be right. The best coaches and leaders have a burning desire to find out what is right, what is the best way. Those who fall short get stuck on it being "their way." Your way may have gotten you here, but what got you here may not always get you there.

Getting to the next level is about working with others to find the best way possible. Admit when you are wrong, pass praise to others as often as you can, and take more accountability and responsibility when things go against you.

ACCEPT RESPONSIBILITY

> *"With great power comes great responsibility."*
>
> **Spider-Man reference**

> *"To whom much is given much is expected."*
>
> **Unknown**

Accepting responsibility for your actions is a common theme on a great team. Being a great leader is not only about taking care of yourself but taking care of your teammates as well. That is an important form of leadership and being a member of a team.

Sometimes our team members fall short of the team's expectations. Sometimes they make mistakes. Sometimes they need a little tough love. Great leaders hold their teammates accountable. They push, challenge and stretch each other to be their best. Don't be afraid to hold your team members accountable. To be effective, you must build trust and a relationship with your team members. If they know you care about them, they will allow you to challenge them and hold them accountable.

Dave Anderson, author of *No-Nonsense Leadership,* said this about being accountable:

> *Leaders must develop a lower threshold for alibis and become better communicators and enforcers of what they want done. If you are more interested in being liked and popular than*

holding people accountable for results, you have a serious leadership weakness. It is not your job to make people happy. Your job is to get them better. Holding people accountable to high standards and results is nothing to apologize for. Failing to stretch them to their potential is.

ENTITLEMENT

A man was walking through the forest and saw a fox that had lost its legs. He couldn't help wondering how it was able to survive.

A few minutes later he saw a tiger come by with some food in its mouth.

The tiger sat down to eat his food. When he had had enough, he left the rest of his food for the fox. The next day, and the day after, the same thing happened. The tiger brought his catch, ate to his desire and left the remainder for the fox.

The man began to wonder: Why do I need to work so hard? Why not just sit back and trust that everything I need will come to me? Why don't I live like the fox and trust that my needs will be taken care of?

And so the next day, the man came back to the forest and sat himself down at the trunk of a tree and did nothing. He placed all his trust in the fact that his needs would be met.

But as days went by, nothing happened — except that the man grew weaker and weaker. By the end of the week he was near death, and in his delirium he heard a clear voice:

"Why did you choose to imitate the disabled fox and not follow the lead of the tiger?"

So many times in life and leadership we want to take the easy road. We feel entitled; we believe that good things should come our way whether or not we earn them.

But leadership is not about entitlement; it's about hard work. To be most effective, you should follow the lead of the tiger in the gifts you bring to those around you. You always have a choice: Sit there lazily and wait for someone else's leftovers, or you can go out and lead.

THREE RULES OF RESPONSE-ABILITY

There are three rules of responsibility taught to me by my mentor Dr. Ken Ravizza, a professor of sport psychology at The California State University, Fullerton and a consultant to top professional athletes and organizations around the world. Dr. Ravizza writes about the rules of response-ability in his groundbreaking book *Heads-Up Baseball*.

1. Before you can control your performance, you must be in control of yourself.

2. You have very little control of what goes on around you, but you have total control over how you choose to respond to it.

3. What you are aware of you can control; what you are unaware of will control you.

Response-ability is the ability to take ownership of your past, command your present and take charge of your future. It is being accountable for your perspective and controlling how you respond to adversity. Too many people are negatively affected by outside influences they cannot control. They respond by becoming a victim of outside factors, rather than responding to adversity by holding themselves responsible for their actions. Most people think that success is learning how to never fail. Success is actually learning from every failure and failing often. Failure is the opportunity to begin again more intelligently. Failure only truly becomes failure when we do not learn from it. In life there are winners and learners. The learners will be around longer than the winners because they will continue to grow and become more.

Perspective is reality, and you are responsible for choosing your attitude and your perspective in any given situation. Attitude is a decision.

THE PROBLEM IS NOT THE PROBLEM

Life is a continuous series of problem-solving events. You are going to have problems and adversity as a leader; that is a given. The problem is not the problem. The problem is how you handle that problem. What is not a given is how you are going to react to problems. It is a choice. You are either going to get frustrated or you are going to get fascinated.

Most people choose frustration - and that doesn't work. It never has; it never will. Fascination always works. Maybe not immediately, but it always works.

It is not always about what happens to you, but how you choose to respond to what happens to you. It is your ability to respond that is going to determine your outcome when adversity is thrown your way. As a human being, you have the ability to respond to an event in the manner you deem appropriate, and the response is your choice.

We often do not have much control over the events in our lives, but we always get to choose our own responses. Choosing your response in any situation is what we call having personal power. Oftentimes your problem isn't the problem. Your reaction to the problem is the problem.

This is an empowering notion because once you realize that you control your response in any situation, you realize you have more control of your life's outcomes than you initially may have thought.

STOP COMPLAINING, "COMPARED TO WHAT"

If you want to get to the next level, you must do one thing: Stop complaining. Quit letting excuses and negativity come out of your mouth. If you complain, you remain the same as the words that are coming out of your mouth at that time. They become your prison bars.

> John Wooden's second set of three guiding principles.
> 1. Don't whine.
> 2. Don't complain.
> 3. Don't make excuses.

Never make excuses. Your friends don't want to hear them, and your opponents won't believe them. "Woe is me" is not the theme song of an excellent leader. You are not a failure until you start blaming others for your mistakes.

While you are in the process of cultivating a better perspective, three of the most powerful words to be conscious of are "Compared to what?" This saying has enormous significance in transforming daunting responsibilities into reasonable tasks. Leaders know how to utilize this question to shift their perspective on the work at hand. They realize that they live in the greatest country in the world. They realize that there are those out there who are less fortunate than they are.

If a negative event occurs and you keep a positive present-moment focus, big-picture mentality and "Compared to what?" perspective as your response, then you will significantly influence the outcome. The reality is that we do not have total control over the outcomes that happen in life; we can only significantly influence.

THE POWER OF "NO"

Your responsibility to the team does not end when you leave practice or a game and engage in activities in your personal life. Part of a leader's responsibility is to say "no" to things that can ultimately affect the team in a negative way. Whether it is peer pressure to attend a party or trying to please everyone, responsible leaders have the ability to say "no."

Many leaders get pulled into more things than they can possibly do, and most of the time it's because they just can't say "no." But the bottom line is that until you start staying "no" to some things, you'll never have time to pursue the really important things. You never want to be disrespectful about it, but you must learn to say "no" if what is asked of you is not a priority. You do have other priorities, and they matter. It's always good to remind people what you're focused on in your sport and in life. Oftentimes, what they want you to do isn't on that list.

Most people don't want to upset or let others down. It's human nature to want to be liked and please others. Some just aren't tough or value-centered enough to say "no." If you think about it, "yes" causes more problems than "no" does.

When you say "no," you may miss an opportunity to go to a party or do things that ultimately may look bad for your team. You won't get in trouble, though. Trouble follows "yes" but rarely "no." You are allowed to be selfish when it comes to being responsible and putting the team before yourself and saying "no."

DWYSYWD

Are you a person of your word? Are your words and actions in line with each other? If you see it, do you own it? When was the last time you picked up a piece of litter on the floor that was not yours and threw it away? If you see it, you own it.

DWYSYWD stands for Do What You Say You Will Do. If you simply do what you say you will do, it puts you ahead of others who, for whatever reason, cannot get the job done and cannot keep their word. They either overcommit, weren't serious enough, don't care enough, don't have the skill of time prioritization down yet, or whatever their excuse-ridden reason may be for breaking their word. Your word is your bond. Your word is one of the most important things you possess, and it makes up your personal credibility and integrity. No one wants to follow a leader who preaches one thing and practices the opposite.

Keeping your word allows people to trust and respect you. It is really hard to have trust in and respect for someone who can't do what they say they will. If you say you are going to do something and it doesn't get done, how is anyone supposed to view you as a leader?

How are your teammates supposed to rely on you as a leader if you can't keep your word? Once trust is compromised, it becomes extremely difficult to regain. It shows maturity when you are able to keep your word, no matter the circumstance. Maturity doesn't come with age; it comes with acceptance of responsibility.

 **COACHING POINT: Think back on the events in your life. Name two specific events that did not go your way. How did you handle those situations of adversity? Did you transfer the blame?**

Or were you accountable for those actions?

Event #1: _____

_____

Response: _____

_____

Event #2: _____

_____

Response: _____

_____

What have you learned about handling situations of adversity?

_____

_____

_____

How will you react to adversity in the future?

_____

_____

_____

4:00 SUMMARY

You will never become the leader you want to be if you keep blaming everyone else for who you are.

Leaders take responsibility, no matter if it's their fault or not.

Before you can control your performance, you must be in control of yourself.

You have very little control of what goes on around you, but you have total control over how you choose to respond to it.

What you are aware of you can control; what you are unaware of will control you.

The problem is not the problem. Your reaction to the problem is the problem.

You have a responsibility to your team to say "NO" sometimes.

DWYSYWD: Do What You Say You Will Do.

4:00 APPLICATION

What are 5 key points you can apply to yourself and
your team from this chapter?

1) _____

2) _____

3) _____

4) _____

5) _____

5:00

POSITIVE ENERGY:
Attitude Is Contagious

> *"Great leaders inflate the people around them. Poor leaders deflate the people around them."*
>
> **Rick Pitino**
> **Head Basketball Coach**
> **University of Louisville**
> **2012-2013 NCAA National Champions**

> *"Nothing great has ever been accomplished without enthusiasm."*
>
> **Ralph Waldo Emerson**

Ken Blanchard, co-author of *The One Minute Manager* and *Leading at a Higher Level*, asks people to do two things at the beginning of his seminars, one of which I attended. First, they greet other people as if they were unimportant. There is usually a dull hum as everyone walks around trying to ignore each other. Then, he stops and asks them to continue to greet people. However, this time do it as if the people they are greeting are long-lost friends they're glad to see. Suddenly, the room erupts with laughter and volume rises as people run around, smiling, laughing and hugging. When the audience sits down Blanchard asks them, "Why do you think I had you do those two things?"

The answer is positive energy. To lead a successful team you must learn to manage the energy of your team, including your own. Was there more energy in the room during the first or second activity? Second. What did he do to change the energy in the room? Simply changing focus from a negative thought to a positive thought increased the energy of the room exponentially.

Why are a positive attitude and positive energy important? Because they are the currency of personal and professional success today. If you don't have that currency, you can't lead, inspire or make as much of a positive difference as you could if you had a positive attitude and energy.

Attitude is not a gene; it is a muscle. It is not something you inherit from family. You understand it, work it, spend time on it and push it - similar to what you would do if you were working out a muscle. If you don't exercise that muscle, the muscle does what? Atrophy. If you don't exercise your positive attitude, what happens to it? It atrophies as well.

Energy is one word that differentiates great leaders from average leaders. Great leaders not only have positive energy, they contagiously spread this positive energy to others. A team filled with pessimism and negativity will find a way to lose, while a team filled with optimism and belief will find a way to win. If you have zest and enthusiasm, you will attract zest and enthusiasm. Negativity thrives in those without a purpose, plan or passion. A positive attitude is like a pair of eyeglasses, a lens through which we view the world. People may hear your words, but they feel your attitude.

> "Keep your thoughts positive because your thoughts become your words.
>
> Keep your words positive because your words become your behavior.
>
> Keep your behavior positive because your behavior becomes your habits.
>
> Keep your habits positive because your habits become your values.
>
> Keep your values positive because your values become your destiny."
>
> **Mahatma Gandhi**

While a positive attitude doesn't always work, a negative attitude always does. Your attitude determines your altitude in life, and attitude is a decision. A leader's attitude will affect the team's mood and altitude. Attitude ultimately reflects leadership. Effort comes before excellence in the dictionary and in life.

Enthusiasm is the same way. Attitude comes before all of them. Attitude is not genetic; it is a muscle that has to be trained. Every single interaction you have with another person leaves that person a little more or a little less energized. Inspire positive energy. To change the world and people's lives we have to be more positive than the negativity we face.

Your conviction (I am) is more powerful than anyone else's prediction (you won't). I am convinced that regardless of task, leaders must be enthusiastic and really enjoy what they are doing if they expect those under their leadership to work near their levels of ability. If you are not fired up with enthusiasm about doing your job, you will be fired with enthusiasm because you will not be very good.

> *A pessimist complains about the wind, an optimist expects the wind to change, but a leader adjusts the sails.*

When I was younger, a positive attitude was not my strong suit. However, I stumbled across a poem that changed my life. I remember it like it was yesterday. I was 14 years old and vacationing with my family in Isle of Palms, South Carolina. We drove to Charleston for the day and ate dinner at Hyman's Seafood Restaurant. As I was flipping through the menu trying to figure out what I wanted to order, I came across this poem that was on the back of the menu. It changed my life:

ATTITUDE

By Charles Swindoll

The longer I live, the more I realize the impact of attitude on life. Attitude to me is more important than facts. It is more important than the past, than education, than money, than circumstances, than failures, than successes, than what other people think, say, or do. It is more important than appearance, giftedness, or skill. It will make or break a company... a team... a home. The remarkable thing is that we have a choice every day regarding the attitude we will embrace for that day. We cannot change our past; we cannot change the fact that people will act in a certain way. We cannot change the inevitable. The one thing we can do is play on the one string we have, and that is our attitude. I am convinced that life is 10% what happens to me and 90% how I react to it. And so it is with you... we are in charge of our attitudes.

After reading that poem, I made a conscious effort to be as positive as I could. Leaders' attitudes are caught by their followers more quickly than their actions. The attitude you take is a decision you make. What kind of attitude will you choose to take today?
Attitude = Altitude.

Attitude is contagious; is yours worth catching?

EAGLES VS. DUCKS

Every team has members who are either ducks or eagles. Ducks are the team members that whine, complain and quack about their situation – the players that think blowing someone else's candle out makes theirs burn brighter. Ducks are the athletes that want the person playing in front of them to get injured so that they can quack into the lineup. They quack about people behind their back and can never be counted on as a great teammate.

Eagles, on the other hand, soar above. They may not like their situation on the team, but they choose to keep their mouths shut and work until their situation improves. They do not participate in backstabbing or locker room lobbying that kills so many teams. Leaders choose a higher road and try to be team builders and confidence creators as opposed to team breakers and confidence destroyers.

FOUNTAINS VS. DRAINS

Like the duck, the drain is an energy vacuum. It sucks out the energy and enthusiasm people have with its destructive tactics. When drains make mistakes, they do not go down alone and often look for other people that they can pull down with them. Drains have a negative effect on other players and teams. They suck the life out of teams.

Fountains provide and spew all the energy. They work to pump up their teammates and carry themselves with a positive energy and attitude regardless of the situation. Fountains may not have their best game that day but are always considered the best teammates to have, because they will always be there to lead everyone else and celebrate the success of others.

The fountain is always part of the answer; the drain is always part of the problem.

The fountain always has a system; the drain has an excuse.

The fountain says, "Let me help you." The drain says, "That's not my job."

The fountain sees an answer for every problem; the drain sees a problem for every answer.

The fountain sees a green near every sand trap; the drain sees two or three sand traps near every green.

The fountain says, "It may be difficult, but it's possible." The drain says, "It may be possible, but it's too difficult."

FEED THE POSITIVE DOG

What we think about we attract. TBT – Thoughts become things. Our thoughts are magnetic. What we think expands and grows. What we focus our energy and attention on starts to show up more in our life.

Remember, whenever there is a dark cloud, there is always sun shining behind it.

> *Where attention goes, energy flows.*

In Jon Gordon's book *The Energy Bus,* he talks about a man going to a faraway village to visit a wise man. Upon arriving, he begins to converse with the wise man. "I feel like there are two dogs inside of me. One is this positive, loving, kind and gentle dog. Then I have this angry, mean-spirited and negative dog, and they fight all the time. I don't know which one is going to win." The wise man thinks for a moment and says, "I know which is going to win - the one you feed the most, so feed the positive dog."

The fact is, we all have a positive and a negative dog inside of us. It's part of our human nature. The key is to feed the positive dog and starve the negative dog. In leadership, overcoming the negative is sometimes more important than the positive. The more we feed the positive, the bigger it gets and the stronger it becomes. The actions are simple. We just need to make them a habit and do them every day.

OVERCOMING ADVERSITY

In *Man's Search for Meaning,* psychologist Viktor Frankl chronicles his experiences as an Auschwitz concentration camp inmate in Nazi Germany during World War II. He documents his attitude for survival, which involved identifying a purpose in life to feel positively about, and then vividly imagining that outcome.

According to Frankl, the way a prisoner imagined the future affected his longevity. He chose to search for something of value and meaning every day of his struggle. He discovered that Nazi officers could take away his family, freedom, food and health; but one certainty they could not take away was his perspective - his ability to choose how he viewed his situation.

Frankl realized that his ability to choose how he responded to his environment was psychological and that his human spirit was free. Knowing this, he found purpose and meaning to every day by aiding fellow prisoners in their fight for survival. When faced with adversity, Frankl chose to change his perspective. Instead of giving in and accepting his fate (which was death), he chose to believe that every person has the ability to choose how he or she responds when faced with adversity. Frankl concluded that the meaning of life is found in every moment of living; life never ceases to have meaning, even in suffering and death.

ADVERSITY IS TO BE EMBRACED

Adversity is inevitable. Everyone deals with it one way or another, but the people who are most effective in dealing with adversity maintain a positive perspective. Perspective is about appreciating what you have and the opportunities before you. Adversity finds everyone; it visits the strong and resides in the weak. Sometimes we get frustrated instead of fascinated with adversity; we give away our response-ability and personal power too easily because we think we are up against insurmountable odds or too tough of a challenge. You don't overcome challenges by making them smaller but by making yourself bigger. Adversity makes you stronger, but only if you resist the temptation to blame something outside of your control for your troubles.

What would you attempt to do if you knew you could not fail?

FAILURE AS FUEL

The topic of failure belongs in the general category of facing adversity. The difference is that failure is viewed as a result, while adversity is seen as something you work your way through. Leadership expert Warren Bennis interviewed 70 of the nation's top performers in various fields and found that none of them viewed their mistakes as failures. They referred to the "failures" as "learning experiences," "tuition paid," "detours" and "opportunities for growth."

Thomas Edison said that he didn't fail repeatedly, he just found 10,000 ways not to make a light bulb. Failure is positive feedback. It provides you with that most direct and unequivocal insight into why and how something has gone wrong. If you are trying to accomplish a task and giving it your best effort, exercising various techniques but are failing, then you are receiving positive feedback from the task on what not to do. This is when you should become fascinated and realize with each attempt you are exposing the details that will lead you to success.

Failure is subjective; you are the only person who can label yourself or what you do a failure. Failure and rejection are the first step to growth. In weight lifting, your muscles are broken down when they are stressed and then built back up, which leads to muscle growth. The same is true for growth through dealing with failure and adversity. The difference between average people and high-achieving people is their perception of and response to failure and adversity.

8 REASONS TO EMBRACE FAILURE

1. Kobe Bryant became the youngest player in NBA history to reach 30,000 career points. He is also on pace to have missed more shots than anyone in history by 2015.

2. Cy Young gave up more hits (7,092) and more earned runs (2,147) than any other pitcher in MLB history. He has won the most games in MLB history (511). He has lost the most games as well (316). The award for the best pitcher in baseball bears his name.

3. Brett Favre threw more interceptions (336), fumbled more times (166), and was sacked more often (525) than any other player in the history of the NFL. He will also go down as one of the best QB's in NFL history and will be inducted into the Hall of Fame.

4. The NBA has never seen a point guard as good as Magic Johnson. However, no one has committed as many turnovers in the playoffs as Magic Johnson has (696).

5. Pete Rose made 10,328 outs in his career. Not the best record to hold, but he does have the most hits in MLB history (4,256) and the most career wins of any

professional athlete or coach in all of professional sports history (1,972).

6. Rickey Henderson was thrown out attempting to steal bases 335 times. That is the most in MLB history. But he also got away with it more than anyone else has (1,406).

7. Wilt Chamberlain is a legend, best remembered for holding the NBA record for points in a game with 100. He missed 5,805 free throws in his career, which is also an NBA record.

8. John Havlicek missed 13,417 shots in his NBA career, more than anyone else to play the game. He also won eight NBA titles and is in the Basketball Hall of Fame.

Failure is not to be avoided. Failure is a necessary part of success.

"Success is not final. Failure is not fatal. It is the courage to continue that counts." – Winston Churchill

HAVE TO VS. GET TO

Oftentimes overcoming adversity has to do with how you perceive a certain situation. By shifting your perception of a situation from negative to positive, you are more likely to achieve a better outcome. One of the perspective challenges facing leaders is a "have-to" vs. "get-to" mentality. All leaders are confronted with these two inescapable perspectives, especially in practice and training. When you say, "I have to," you are giving in to a negative energy generated by the feeling of some external obligation, which manifests a negative attitude.

As a leader, you must turn your "have to's" into "get to's" whenever you recognize yourself feeling obligated to perform. When you use "get to," your energy and attitude move into a positive perspective. A feeling of personal preference generates this, when you feel in control of yourself and enjoy what you are doing.

COMPARED TO WHAT?

The phrase "Compared to what?" is a perspective change that has enormous significance for transforming daunting undertakings into reasonable tasks. Leaders know how to utilize this question to shift their perspective on the work at hand. They learn, when faced with the prospect of a challenge, to take a moment to reflect and ask "compared to what?" Leaders realize the world is full of people that are less fortunate than they. The importance of perspective is premised on the fact that no matter how difficult a situation you are in, someone has it worse.

For example, if you are a college student and you don't want to go to class or study, compare yourself to persons who are earning minimum wage because they didn't have the opportunity to go to college and instead had to provide for their families at an early age. What about an athlete who feels tired and doesn't want to practice or lift weights, compared to the soldier who is stationed in hostile territory and has to get up for a lookout shift so that we can participate in athletics and life in a free country?

University of Alabama-Birmingham head baseball coach Brian Shoop, one of the most amazing men and best leaders I have ever met, uses a "Compared to what?" mentality with his team to help them build perspective:

You know, we are the wealthiest society here in America, and I read that studies say that we're the 16th happiest. So money and material things must not translate into happiness. We are also a society that complains way too much. You have nations that don't have food, and we complain if it takes too long to get to our table at the restaurant. We complain we didn't get perfect service from a waitress that might be having a real tough issue at home.

We're asking the wrong questions. Our facilities are not the best in the country, but we have everything we need to be champions. If we'll choose to be thankful for what we do have instead of complaining about what we don't have, life's a heck of a lot better.

YET = DELAYED SUCCESS

By adding YET to the end of your sentence, you leave the door open to performance excellence and response to adversity as opposed to slamming it in your own face. When presented with a difficult task, how do you respond?

There are two ways to look at that question: I can't do it, it's too hard = Failure. You haven't even given yourself a chance for success. However, I can't do that....yet = Delayed success.

When you add YET to the end of your sentence, you are telling yourself "when this happens....." instead of "if this happens...." YET is also an acronym for Your Energy Talks. When the mood is down and thoughts are negative, use this acronym to remind yourself and others to change the outlook on the situation.

 COACHING POINT: Out of all the tasks you accomplish throughout the day, list the three you enjoy the most and the three you enjoy the least. Three most enjoyable tasks:

1) _____

2) _____

3) _____

Three least enjoyable tasks:
1) _____

2) _____

3) _____
Which of your responsibilities do you enjoy the least? Are these expectations from others or duties you have created for yourself? How can you develop enthusiasm to complete less-than-enjoyable tasks, particularly the ones over which you have no control?

1) _____

2) _____

3) _____

PERSEVERANCE

It is a rare person who doesn't get discouraged in the face of adversity. Whether it happens to you or to a teammate, the answer to overcoming adversity lies in one word: PERSEVERANCE. Courage, persistence and perseverance are topics you hear in sports and in life. One man illustrated these concepts better than anyone throughout history. His age appears in the column on the right to better illustrate what perseverance is all about.

ADVERSITY	AGE
Failed in business	22
Ran for Legislature - defeated	23
Failed again in business	24
Elected to Legislature	25
Death of wife	26
Nervous breakdown	27
Defeated for Speaker	29
Defeated for Elector	31

Defeated for Congress	34
Elected to Congress	37
Defeated for Congress	39
Defeated for Senate	46
Defeated for Vice President	47
Defeated for Senate	49
Elected President of the United States	51

Who is that man, you ask? None other than the 16th President of The United States of America, Abraham Lincoln. You may be disappointed if you fail, but you are doomed if you don't try. Failure is not in losing, but in not getting up off the mat when you get knocked down.

 **COACHING POINT: How do you respond to adversity? What are specific examples of times when you have fought back in the face of adversity?**

_____

_____

5:00 SUMMARY

Great leaders not only have positive energy, they contagiously spread this positive energy to others.

Leaders who are most effective in dealing with adversity maintain a positive perspective.

Be a fountain, not a drain.

Feed the positive dog.

Failure is not to be avoided; it is a necessary part of success.

As a leader, you must turn your "have to's" into "get to's."

"Compared to what?" is a perspective change that has enormous significance for transforming daunting undertakings into reasonable tasks.

By adding YET to the end of your sentence, you leave the door open to performance excellence and response to adversity as opposed to slamming it in your own face.

YET also stands for Your Energy Talks.

The answer to overcoming adversity is perseverance.

5:00 APPLICATION

What are 5 key points you can apply to yourself and your team from this chapter?

1) _____

2) _____

3) _____

4) _____

5) _____

6:00

EMOTIONAL CONTROL:
Emotion Clouds Reality

Much like Tiger Woods today, Bobby Jones was a golf legend. He began playing golf in 1907. He was only five years old and already a child golf prodigy. When he was only 12, he was shooting below par, better than professionals over twice his age. At 14, he qualified for the United States Amateur Championship. He went on to lose the event but he earned a nickname, which would best describe his problem: Club Thrower.

He struggled with controlling his temper, therefore losing his ability to perform well. He was advised by a friend of his family to harness his emotions. "You'll never win until you can control that temper of yours," the man said. Jones soon mastered his emotions and became one of the best golfers of his era, maybe even of history. He retired at the age of 28, after winning the grand slam of golf. Soon thereafter, Jones' family friend made this comment: "Bobby was fourteen when he mastered the game of golf, but he was twenty-one when he mastered himself."

In the heat of competition, it is easy for your mind to become clouded by anger and negative emotions. It is easy to let emotions get the best of your performance. When you take emotion out of the picture, you tend to respond more clearly. What does emotion do in life and athletic performance? It clouds reality.

SPORTS IS NOT LIFE OR DEATH

Often leaders can make the mistake of approaching insignificant situations as if they were life and death, not their job or sport. Most of the time there is much regret that emotions overpowered sensible response-ability. ***You must be in control of yourself before you control your performance.*** Relax, recover and gain control of your thoughts, feelings and emotions.

A prime example of a leader losing their cool is former Ohio State University Football Coach Woody Hayes punching a Clemson player in the 1978 Gator Bowl On December 29, 1978. Late in the fourth quarter, the Tigers were leading the Buckeyes 17–15. Freshman quarterback Art Schlichter drove the Buckeyes down the field into field goal range. On 3rd and 5 at the Clemson 24-yard line with 2:30 left and the clock running, Hayes called a pass and the pass was intercepted by Clemson nose guard Charlie Bauman, who returned it toward the OSU sideline where he was run out of bounds.

After Bauman rose to his feet, Hayes punched him in the throat, starting a bench-clearing brawl. Hayes stormed onto the field and was abusive to the referee. When one of Hayes' own players, offensive lineman Ken Fritz, tried to intervene, Hayes turned on him and had to be restrained by defensive coordinator George Hill. This would be the last game Woody Hayes would coach in college football.

Great leaders are able to keep their emotions in check during the heat of battle. They effectively manage their emotions and keep themselves on an even keel when everyone and everything else around them might be going crazy. Why is it so important to manage your emotions? Because the people you lead will be watching you to see how you handle the situation. Whatever response you show, they will be likely to reflect the same response.

Sports arouse emotions and passions like no other endeavor. Our attitudes, belief systems and thoughts create our reality. They also create our emotions. Joy is one, pride is another. The others are anger and fear. Emotions, particularly anger, are like fire. They can cook your food and keep you warm, or they can burn your house down. It is easy to respond out of anger without thought or control.

When you let anger get the best of you, it usually brings out the worst in you. The best leaders are masters of their emotions and not servants to them. Buy the solution, not the emotion.

To become our best, good judgment and common sense are essential. No matter the task – whether physical or mental – if our emotions take over, we're not going to execute near our personal levels of competency because both judgment and common sense will be impaired. When our emotions dominate our lives, we make mistakes.

THE INVERTED U OF SELF-CONTROL

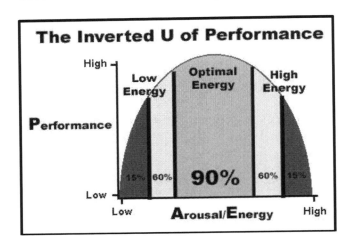

To be in control of your performance, you first have to control yourself. Gaining self-control and optimal performance can best bet understood by the Inverted U of Performance. When your arousal/energy goes up so does your performance. When you get to fired up, to energized your performance will suffer just as it will when your energy is too low. To give yourself the best chance for success your energy and self-control must be in an optimal place. This is best achieved by having daily performance routines that will help you to stay consistent.

POOL SHARK ANALOGY

As a mental conditioning coach for one of the best billiards players in the world, I learned a critical emotional management strategy that pool sharks use in competition. When they make a shot, they always step back from the table, chalk their stick, take a deep breath and recalculate their next best course of action before stepping back to the table. We must do the same when we are under stress and have strong emotions. We must step away from the leadership table, chalk our sticks and take a deep breath before choosing our next best course of action.

GOLF ANALOGY

Think of it as the golf swing principle. If we swing to hit a golf ball with a lot of emotion, the ball will be even further out to the right or left than it would be if we swung with self-control. Even the PGA golf professionals I work with will tell you that an emotional swing will yield a non-desired result.

Lack of self-control not only hinders individual achievement, but it also hinders team accomplishment.

4 WAYS PEOPLE DEAL WITH EMOTION

Tony Robbins, life coach, self-help author and motivational speaker, talks about the four ways that people deal with emotions in his book *Re-awaken the Giant Within:*

1. Avoidance: We all want to avoid painful emotions. As a result, most people try to avoid any situation that could lead to the emotions that they fear — or worse, some people try not to feel any emotions at all! A much more powerful approach is to learn to find the hidden, positive meaning in those things you once thought were negative emotions.

2. Denial: Experiencing an emotion and trying to pretend it's not there only creates more pain. Once again, ignoring the messages that your emotions are trying to give you will not make things better. If the message your emotions are trying to deliver is ignored, the emotions simply increase their power; they intensify until you finally pay attention. Trying to deny your emotions is not the solution. Understanding and harnessing them is the strategy.

3. Competition: Many people stop fighting their painful emotions and decide to fully indulge in them. Rather than learn the positive message their emotion is trying to give them, they intensify it and make it even worse than it is. It literally becomes part of their identity, a way of being unique; they begin to pride themselves on being worse off than anyone else. As you can imagine, this is one of the deadliest traps of all.

This approach must be avoided at all costs, because it becomes a self-fulfilling prophecy where the person ends up having an investment in feeling bad on a regular basis — and then he/she is truly trapped. A much more powerful and healthy approach to dealing with the emotions that we think are painful is to realize that they serve a positive purpose.

4. Learning and Using: If you want to make your life really work, you must make your emotions work for you. You can't run from them; you can't tune them out; you can't trivialize them or delude yourself about what they mean. Nor can you just allow them to run your life. Emotions, even those that seem painful in the short term, are truly like an internal compass that points you toward the actions you must take to arrive at your goals.

ACT DIFFERENTLY THAN HOW YOU FEEL

As the leader, you cannot allow your "gray" days to show. If you do, others' perceptions of what you're thinking or feeling will become their reality. Pessimism and doubt are simply not an option as a leader. You must learn to have good bad days.

No matter what worries or concerns are on your mind, you are always the one who people look to for direction and assurance. Your team needs to know that "we're going to get there" and that a game plan exists to make that belief a reality, especially when things are not going your way. The difference between who you are and who you want to be is what you do.

The concept of acting differently than how you feel, and faking it till you make it, will change your perspective and help you to start turning your bad days into good bad days.

ACTING – FEELING - THINKING

It is easier to act your way into feeling and thinking than it is to think and feel your way into action. When you act the way you want to feel, you dramatically increase your chances of finding the energy and emotion you need to lead your team because, in time, you are going to start to feel the way you have been acting. Do what you should do, regardless of how you feel.

The concept of ACE (Acting Changes Everything) builds upon the previous idea that you are an actor as well as a leader. You must commit yourself to this belief because acting changes everything. It changes your perception of your situation and the perception others have of you.

PERCEPTION IS REALITY

One of the greatest examples of this concept is Game Five of the 1997 NBA Finals. Bitten hard by the flu bug, Michael Jordan was so ill some speculated that he wouldn't be able to play in Game 5 against the Utah Jazz in Utah with the series tied at 2-2. The Bulls' medical staff told Jordan there was no way he could play that night. As one of the greatest competitors and leaders in the history of sports, he refused to accept a role on the sidelines. Jordan fought the Jazz, feeling the effects of dehydration and exhaustion (he could barely walk to the bench during timeouts), and won. Jordan turned in a masterful performance with 38 points and seven rebounds, sending the series back to Chicago with the Bulls up 3-2. Two days later, the Bulls won their fifth NBA World Championship in six years.

In Game 5 of the 1997 NBA Finals, Michael Jordan was forced to act differently than how he felt. If he hadn't, he might not have played that night, costing the Bulls a shot at an NBA Championship. What Jordan understood was that acting changes everything. It motivates both oneself and others, while changing perceptions of possibility.

EQ

One of the mistakes leaders often make is trying to take a "cookie-cutter" approach to leadership. The only problem with that is every person is different and doesn't respond to the same type of leadership. You should treat everyone with consistency and respect. However, the same leadership style and strategies you use for one person may not work for the next person. Being a leader is more than strategy; it involves a true understanding of your emotions and those around you. Without this, bad communication, misunderstandings and mistakes can be made.

One person might need to be challenged while another may need to be encouraged. Some may need the game plan drawn up for them; others will help develop the plan. If you want to be the best leader you can be, you need to be able to adapt to the situation and what your people need at that time. They shouldn't be expected to adapt to you.

We often hear about intelligence quotient (IQ), or how smart you are. Your emotional quotient, or EQ, is different because instead of measuring your general intelligence, it measures your emotional intelligence. Emotional quotient is the ability to sense, understand and apply the power and judgment of emotions to assist in developing high levels of teamwork and productivity.

Outside of athletics, emotional intelligence is important because it helps you control your awareness of emotions for effectiveness in the workplace. In the athletic arena, emotional intelligence is about having a "feel," an awareness, for who you need to be as a leader at a given time.

Think of yourself as a chameleon with the ability to adapt and adjust to change the color of your skin for a given situation. Don't mistake that for not being true to yourself; it is you being a leader, being in control of yourself and the team, and being the highest level of serving professional.

Part of what makes leaders so effective is that they can act in a way that is needed in a certain situation. If you need to act compassionate, act compassionate. If you need to be stern, be stern. If you need to act disciplined, act disciplined. Do you need to be high-energy? Then be high-energy. Your values will always guide what you do, and you also must understand who you need to be in the moment and get a pulse from your team.

Emotional control is all about being who you need to be when you need to be that person, to give yourself the best chance for success, regardless of how you feel.

THINK BEFORE YOU SPEAK (OR PRESS SEND)

One problem that leaders may have is not thinking before they say something and speaking out of emotion. If emotions of life or a game get the best of you and you overreact, you must be able to tame your tongue. It's better to bite your tongue than to eat your words.

Legendary University of Michigan Football Coach Bo Schembechler used to say that "loose lips sink ships." Not being in control of your emotions and words not only looks bad on you, but on everyone important around you. The first step to improve is to think before you say something that you may later regret. What we say and later regret often comes out of our mouths when we are in an emotional state.

The next time you think about lashing out, take a deep breath and think: "How will this affect my life, my coaches, my teammates, my family, my school, my relationships, etc.?" By doing this, you give yourself a chance to cool down and look at things more rationally. You also take emotion out of it and look through a clearer lens of focus. Remember, when you say something that damages the character and reputation of those associated with you, you can never take it back. People may forgive what you say, but they will never forget how it made them feel. Sticks and stones may break bones. Bones will heal; it is the words that you use that can leave scars forever.

Gossip among a team is a killer.

What you put in writing is permanent and can be used against you and your reputation. This goes for social media as well - Twitter and Facebook especially. When you think about posting to a social media account, ask yourself how it is going to affect those in your inner circle. It is the same concept as spoken words. Always think before pressing send. How many times have you spoken something out loud or on social media that you like to take back? I would say most of us have been in that situation. It could have easily been avoided if you stopped, took a deep breath, and asked yourself how it would affect those who have a vested interest in your well-being. Then, once you do those things and decide only positives can come out of this, it is OK to speak the words or post on social media accounts.

COACHING POINT: Describe three encounters in which you have seen emotions hinder clear thinking.

1) _____

2) _____

3) _____

What areas of your life can present the greatest difficulty in gaining and maintaining control of your emotions?

1) _____

2) _____

In what areas of your life do you present the most control of your emotions?

1) _____

2) _____

6:00 SUMMARY

When you let anger get the best of you, it usually brings out the worst in you.

The best leaders are masters of their emotions and not servants to them.

Great leaders are able to keep their emotions in check during the heat of battle.

To be in control of your performance, you first have to control yourself.

It is easier to act your way into feeling and thinking than it is to think and feel your way into action.

Emotional control is all about being who you need to be when you need to be that person to give yourself the best chance for success.

Think how your words will affect you and those closest to you before speaking or pressing send.

6:00 APPLICATION

What are 5 key points you can apply to yourself and your team from this chapter?

1) _____

2) _____

3) _____

4) _____

5) _____

PART III

LEARNING TO LEAD

7:00

LEAD VERBALLY AND BY EXAMPLE:

Communication Is Key

> *"People need a model to see more than they need a motto to say."*
>
> **Steve Smith**
> **Head Baseball Coach**
> **Baylor University**

In the #1 New York Times best-selling book and hit movie, *Lone Survivor*, U.S. Navy SEALs take part in Operation Redwing. This operation consisted of a team of four Navy SEALs, tasked for surveillance and reconnaissance of a compound being used by Afghan militia and their leader Ahmad Shah. Shah was responsible for killing a group of Marines just weeks prior. The team's location was soon compromised, as a group of goat herders stumbled upon their position.

They had a decision to make: Kill the men, take them hostage, or let them go and have their safety compromised. So they took a vote, with everyone able to voice their opinion of the goat herders' fate. In an extremely courageous act of leadership, it was decided that the men should be released because the rules of engagement said so. Even though not all members voted for that outcome, team leader Michael Murphy took a stand and made a confident decision. He thought it was in the best interest of his team and country to let these men go. His verbal leadership and leadership by example were respected by his teammates.

Just as they had predicted, their location was compromised. SEAL Team 10 fell into an ambush by Shah and his group just hours after inserting into the area by MH-47 helicopter. Three of the four SEALs were killed, and a Quick Reaction Force helicopter sent in for their aid was shot down with an RPG-7 rocket-propelled grenade, killing all eight Navy SEALs and all eight U.S. Army Special Operations aviators on board.

Throughout the situation, the lone survivor (Marcus Luttrell) and his three teammates (team leader and Navy Lieutenant Michael P. Murphy, Petty Officer Second Class Danny P. Dietz, and Petty Officer Second Class Matthew G. Axelson) were involved in extremely hostile conditions. Gunfights lasted for hours, all while attempting to navigate treacherous mountain terrain. However, their leadership, both verbally and by example, was heroic.

Badly wounded and surrounded by Afghan militia, the men had no choice but to stick together to survive. Their motto was, "You are never out of the fight." Throughout the battle, each member would check in to see how the other members were holding up, knowing they were badly wounded. No matter the situation, they were going to continue to fight. At one point, Dietz said to Luttrell, "Marcus, I'm shot, I'm shot." Luttrell's response was, "We have all been shot, but can you fight?" This is a true testament to how courageous these men were. Their verbal leadership and the example they set for the other men on the team were extraordinary.

MUST LEAD VERBALLY
AND WITH ACTIONS

Many people think that leaders lead either by example or verbally. This is true. Most leaders have a preferred leadership style. However, if you are only leading verbally or by example, you are only a 50% leader. 50% is a FAILING GRADE.

Great leaders lead both by example and verbally. If you do not do both, you are only half of a leader. You must do both to be a true leader and maximize your leadership influence.

It is an excuse for mediocrity and fear of getting out of your comfort zone, used by many, to say you are one and not the other. To have loyal followers, they must see and hear their leader being consistent in action and word. The greater their consistency in action and word, the greater the loyalty of their followers.

What people hear, they understand. What they see, they believe.

PSYCHOLOGY & PHYSIOLOGY CONNECTION

Your psychology will affect your physiology and your physiology will affect your psychology. Watching the way a person walks and listening to the way a person talks tells you a lot about the person's belief about getting the job done. Real leadership is being the person others want to follow because your words, actions and values all align. If you wouldn't follow yourself, why would anyone else?

COMMUNICATION

Alabama head football coach Nick Saban stresses the importance of communication to his players. He had this to say about the importance of communication:

> *I just think that in this day and age, the players are a little less geared toward communicating. They do a lot of texting, they do a lot of Facebook, they do a lot of social media; but in doing that, they don't spend as much time communicating with other people.*
>
> *That's one of the things that we really try to emphasize: that we have good communication.*

During a leadership seminar with his team, Saban's first question to his players was, "Do you think it's important to tell your teammates what you think?" 95% of the guys said *No*. Most of the answers were something like "That's for the coach to do, or the strength coach or somebody in a position of authority."

The next question asked of the players was, "What's the most important thing - to you - about your teammates?" The unanimous answer was, "What they think of me." This gives you a sense of how much of a disconnect there is in the importance of communication.

Leadership rises and falls with communication. Never forget that because you are the leader, your communication sets the tone for the interaction among your people. The greatest leaders are highly skilled communicators, both verbally and by example.

THREE STANDARDS TO LEAD YOUR TEAM:

1. Be decisive: Nothing frustrates team members more than leaders who can't make up their minds and make a decision.
2. Be clear: Your team cannot execute if the members don't know what you want. Don't try to dazzle anyone with your intelligence; impress people with your straightforwardness and simplicity.
3. Be respectful: Everyone deserves to be shown respect, no matter what position they hold. By being respectful, you set the tone for the entire organization.

Great leaders always have a "why" for everything they do or don't. They will always give an explanation. Many leaders will bark orders, but the best leaders will tell you the problem and let you know how to fix it and why it needs fixing.

THE POWER OF WHY

Legendary University of Indiana Basketball Coach Bobby Knight is a big proponent of WHY. He says that a crucial element in communicating the message to others is "why." "In teaching and evaluating, I always tell them why."

University of North Carolina Basketball Coach Roy Williams agrees with Knight. He strives to teach the reasons behind every action, every drill, every evaluation. He explains to his team why and clearly states the purpose for everything they do.

Former NFL football coach Herm Edwards believes that communicating to players why they are doing something, rather than just ordering them to do it, allows them to take ownership of what they are trying to accomplish individually and as a team.

> *Knowing why allows the players to trust what we are doing, and when they trust it, they won't question it under stress.*

MODELING LEADERSHIP

In John Maxwell's book *Developing the Leaders Around You*, noted medical missionary Albert Schweitzer is quoted as saying, "Example is not the main thing in influencing others; it is the only thing."

Modeling leadership is essential in creating an appealing climate for growing potential leaders. People mimic what they see modeled. Positive model-positive response. Negative model-negative response. What leaders do, followers around them do. What they value, their teammates value. The leaders' goals become their goals. Leaders set the tone and provide the pulse for the team. As a leader, you need to remember that when you have followers, they can only go as far as you take them. If you stop growing, your ability to lead will stop as well. We cannot model what we don't possess. Continue to grow while growing those around you.   If you are not growing, you are dying.

PYRAMID OF LEADERSHIP

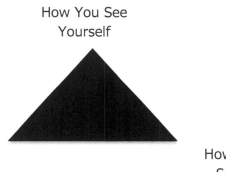

How You See
Yourself

How Do You
Want To Be
Seen?

How Others
See You

1. How you want to be seen: This is how you live your life and see yourself in the moment.   If you are evaluating yourself accurately and want to be the right type of leader, people will see you that way.

2. How you see yourself: This is where you create the vision of how you want to be seen as a leader.   It requires accurate self-evaluation and awareness.   You have to take a look inside yourself and see yourself as a leader that puts the team ahead of the individual.

3. How other people see you: This is the most important part of the pyramid and often the toughest to measure by yourself.   That is why you need 360° feedback from coaches and from other people in your organization about how they see you.

If how you see yourself and how you want to be seen are different from how other people see you, your self-analysis is off. You may see yourself as a great leader, but if others don't follow you, then you are not a leader - you are simply going for a walk.

 COACHING POINT: What are some strengths that you currently possess as a verbal leader?

_____

_____

What are some things you need to work on to become better at leading verbally?

_____

_____

What are some good things you currently do to lead by example?

_____

_____

What are some things you need to work on to become better at leading by example?

_____

7:00 SUMMARY

If you are only leading verbally or by example, you are only a 50% leader. 50% is a FAILING GRADE.

People need a model to see more than a motto to say.

You must lead verbally and with your actions.

Leadership rises and falls with communication.

3 standards to lead your team: Be decisive. Be clear. Be respectful.

Always give people a reason "WHY."

Your followers can only go as far as you take them.

You may see yourself as a great leader, but if others don't follow you, then you are not a leader - you are simply going for a walk.

7:00 APPLICATION

What are 5 key points you can apply to yourself and your team from this chapter?

1) _____

2) _____

3) _____

4) _____

5) _____

8:00

FOCUS ON THE PROCESS:
Destination is the Disease, Journey is the Reward

Yesterday is history, tomorrow is a mystery, and today is a gift - that's why it is called the present.

If you were to drive from New York City to Los Angeles, and if you left at midnight and the sun never came up until you arrived, could you still drive across the country?

Yes, you could.

Headlights are what will allow you to see your path. Although headlights do not extend from the East Coast to the West Coast, they do let you see the next 200 feet of road. What you are to do is drive the next 200 feet over and over again until you get to your final destination.

For the high school coach looking to repeat a season as state champions or the college coach looking to win your next NCAA championship, the task is the same. Focus on the next 200 feet and be relentless in your pursuit of excellence on a daily basis. Stick with the process, stay positive in your approach, control what you can control, and let the results take care of themselves.

How do you eat an elephant? One bite at a time. How did Sir Edmund Hillary climb Mt. Everest? One step at a time. Step by step creates a path, stone by stone creates a cathedral. Inch by inch it is a cinch, yard by yard it is hard.

During the 2013 Heisman Trophy Ceremony, Alabama quarterback AJ McCarron was asked how he manages to handle every situation thrust before him throughout the year. With all of the success and media attention, how does he stay focused on the task at hand? His answer: "By living in the moment and having fun."

During the same Heisman Trophy Ceremony, Florida State quarterback Jameis Winston, the Heisman winner, referenced the process eight times during his acceptance speech. Trust in the process is what he said has allowed him to achieve success so far in life and athletics. By trusting in the process, Jameis Winston has developed into one of the top collegiate athletes in the country.

When we live in the moment and focus on the process and not the destination or the outcome, we provide our team the best chance for success. Legendary LSU Baseball Coach Skip Bertman, who won five NCAA National Championships in the 1990's, was a big believer in the process. Bertman said there were only four outcomes that could happen in a baseball game, and he referred to these four outcomes as The Law of Averages.

THE LAW OF AVERAGES

1. Your team can play well and win.
2. Your team can play well and lose.
3. Your team can play poorly and win.
4. Your team can play poorly and lose.

Bertman used the law of averages to his advantage. His thought was that if you play your best, you give yourself the best chance to win, but you are not guaranteed to win. You do not have control over the outcome of the game. The process of performing excellently was what won games, not a focus on winning games.

Bertman understood that focusing on the scoreboard could be devastating to a team. Instead, when you focus on the process of performing at your best, you give yourself the best chance to win, knowing that it may not happen because you cannot control the outcome.

FOCUS ON PROCESS, NOT OUTCOME

Destination is the disease, journey is the reward.

Destination disease is when I get THERE, my job will be better; when I get THERE, my career will be better. How do you cure destination disease? By focusing on the next 200 feet. Our society has been saturated by a mindset of instant gratification and winning right now. Simply put, people are impatient and want it faster, cheaper and easier. Burger King, anyone?

We as a society want too much too soon and have forgotten that the value of accomplishment is in direct proportion to the effort given to achieve the accomplishment.

In life, the biggest and most significant accomplishments take time. Usually the better the reward, the more time investment is required. Most people think that success is instantaneous. They look at it as a moment, an event or a place in time. It's not. Success is really a process. It is growth and development. It is achieving one thing and using that as a stepping-stone to achieve something else. It is a journey.

> *"Success is not something you pursue. Success is something that you attract by becoming a successful person."*
> **Jim Rohn**

We live in a results-driven society. An excellent process will give you excellent results. By performing a step-by-step process directed at excellence, you will get to the peak of your mountain of success one step at a time.

Leaders must understand that winning is the result of performance excellence - being at your best, every day.

Do not be daunted by your destination. You chose it because you want it: because a fiery passion within you burns and craves to shed its light on the snowcapped peak of your mountain. You will achieve excellence, but in due time.

RUN YOUR MARATHON

Take the example of running a marathon. It can be an extremely daunting task. However, if you become immersed in the process, you give yourself the best chance for success during those 26.2 miles. Instead of focusing on the fact that you have to run 26.2 miles, focus on the process of running the best one mile you can 26 times.

PATIENCE IN THE PROCESS

Patience is a virtue. It is the ability to wait and calmly persevere. We all grow impatient, but some people have more trouble waiting than others do. We tend to forget that all good things take time. The element of time adds value to the accomplishment. We shouldn't expect things to happen overnight. Actually, getting something too easily or too soon can cheapen the outcome. If you believe enough in the process, success will come to you. You must be willing to see it through to the end.

THE PENALTY OF YOUTH

Youth can be impatient. Young people have the tendency to want to change more things more quickly. The mistake they make is that they see all change as progress, and they fail to see the benefit of waiting. Major League Baseball teams understand the amount of time and patience needed to produce players of Major League caliber. Most Major League players spend years coming up through minor league systems. According to *Business Insider*, three years after a particular draft takes place you will probably only see about 15% of that year's draftees in the Major Leagues. And for most players, it will take four to six years to make it to the highest level.

This principle of paying your dues is not only found in baseball, but it's part of the business world, the educational system and most other areas of life. Patience, knowledge and experience all come before success. The maxim "easy come, easy go" carries more truth in it than most people realize. When we add to our accomplishments the element of hard work over a long period of time, we'll place far greater value on the outcome. When we are patient, we'll have a greater appreciation of our success.

 COACHING POINT: What aspects of the process in your sport or your life, if focused on, would give you the greatest chance to perform at your best?

_____

_____

WHAT IS VS. WHAT IF

Imagine if someone asked you to walk across a plank of wood that was sitting on the ground. Would you have a problem doing that? Probably not. What if the same person raised that board and laid it across two chairs? A little tougher, but still no fear of falling. Now, imagine that I stretched a board across the Grand Canyon and told you to walk across. No, thank you.

What thoughts would you have?

How would you feel?

Could you do it?

The task is the same, so what is the difference? If you approach the board over the Grand Canyon with a "what is" attitude, you realize it is the same as the board that is on the ground. The "what if" attitude that many of us get when we face adversity or get out of our comfort zone makes you focus on all the things that could go wrong in walking across the board.

Many of us fall into the trap of thinking about "what if" this happens or "what if" that happens. We focus on things outside of our control and we lose focus on the process. This is the same mindset people have in competition. Great leaders have the ability to focus on "what is" and spread that to those around them. When you focus on "what is," you are living in the present; but when you focus on "what if," you are living with one foot in the past and one foot in the future and popping a squat, aka going to the bathroom all over the present.

IN VS. INTO

An elderly carpenter was ready to retire. He told his employer of his plans to leave the contracting business and live a more relaxed, leisurely life with his family. He would miss the paycheck, but he needed to move on to do something else. His family would be OK financially.

His employer was sorry to see his good worker go. Before he went, his boss asked him if he could build just one more house as a personal favor. The carpenter agreed to build, but it was easy to see that his heart was not fully into his work. He resorted to poor workmanship and used low-grade materials in the last house he would ever build. It was an unfortunate way to finish an accomplished career.

When the carpenter completed his work, the employer came to inspect it. He handed the keys to the carpenter. "This is your house," he said. "It is my gift to you." The carpenter was shocked. What a shame. If only he had known he was building his own house, he would have done it so differently. He would've built with passion, pride, commitment, discipline and attention to detail. He would have known that doing something nearly right and doing it exactly right is usually the difference between success and failure.

So it is with us as athletes, coaches and people. We build our lives one day at a time. We often put less than our best effort into the building. Then, with a shock, we realize we have to live in the house we have built. If we could do it over, we would do it much differently, but we cannot go back and build a new foundation that has already been set.

Leadership is a do-it-yourself project. Others will be there to help, but getting your team where they desire to go starts with you. Your attitude and the choices you make daily build the house that you will live in tomorrow.

Leaders in all aspects of sport and life recognize a substantial difference between being "in" versus "into" your performance. As you are reading this section, I want you to experience the difference between being in and being into the process of becoming a great leader by asking yourself the following questions:

Are you reading this manual because someone wanted you to?

Are you reading this because you want to be a better leader?

As you read, are you highlighting or underlining text you feel is important?

Are you taking notes in the margins?

Are you fully engaged in the process or are you just reading along?

Are you just "in" or are you "into" reading this book?

People who possess an "in" mindset go through the motions or are doing things because other people want them to. They feel as if they "have to" and only last for so long before being replaced by people who possess the "into" mentality.

Those who are truly "into" are driven by a purpose. Being "into" means you are doing something because you want to, and you are passionate about your performance because you want to be at your very best.

W.I.N. – WHAT'S IMPORTANT NOW

You will get distracted because everyone does. The achievement of being a successful leader depends on the development of distraction awareness. You must develop the ability to recognize when you are distracted and then refocus back into the moment. Here is an easy way to remember this: If I want to win or achieve success, I must focus on "What's Important Now."

Focus on what you are doing right here in this moment and on accomplishing the task in the moment. There is an old saying that says you should be where your feet are. What that means is this: Focus on the process and what's important now, today. Don't focus on where you were yesterday or where you'll be tomorrow. That is taking your focus away from how successful you could be today. This is the focus of successful leaders and successful progress. Don't let the same team beat you twice. Don't let yesterday take up too much of today.

To be a great player is not to compete with anyone else, whether it's your predecessor, a peer or a role model. You've got to play your own game. Your focus has to be 100 percent on what matters most - the shot, swing, pitch, throw or catch you are about to make. The same is true for leaders, who cannot afford to be distracted by outside forces that allow one's ego to get involved. What matters most is the team - where it is headed and the team's ability to get there. It is about getting your teammates to focus on W.I.N. That's the next pitch that's being thrown, the next play that is being run or the next shot being taken. It is all about the here and now.

SUM OF "TODAYS"

Today + today + today + today = your life and your career. The future is just a bunch of what-you-do-right-nows strung together. Your career is really the sum of all of your "todays." Many of us get caught up in counting the days until the big game or just going through the motions of practice, thinking that we are "gamers" and can turn it on when it counts and get the job done. Don't count the days; make the days count!

DON'T COUNT THE DAYS

The first step to making your days count is to focus on the process and avoid destination disease. The future and destination are just a bunch of what-you-do-right-nows strung together. Success in any sport and life is really the sum of our todays. You must challenge yourself to make each day your masterpiece. Don't ruin a good today by thinking about a bad yesterday.

RELEASE YOUR MENTAL BRICKS

How much does a standard brick weigh? Roughly 5 pounds. If I asked you to carry a standard brick around for 5 seconds, could you do it? Yes, it would not be that difficult. What if you carry that same brick for 5 minutes? Slightly tougher but still doable. What about 5 hours? Now it starts to become a little more difficult, if not impossible.

As coaches, athletes and leaders, most of us, if we have a bad play, a bad day of practice or a bad game, carry a lot of "mental bricks." Those mental bricks build up, weigh on us and zap our energy similar to what it may be like to physically carry a brick all day.

Releasing mental bricks is a concept for leaders to get back into the present moment and to let go of failure and negativity that are built into competition.

Imagine that I told you to wear a weighted vest from the time you woke up until the time you went to sleep. You had to go through the entire day without taking the vest off. You had to sit through classes, walk through campus, perform in practice, go to study hall - everything - with that vest on. By the end of the day you would be physically and probably mentally exhausted. That is the best example of what carrying mental bricks is really like. It completely drains your energy level and hinders you in focusing on the process. Instead of setting your sights on who you need to become to lead and help your team become successful, you are focusing on things that are out of your control and that you should not be concerned with.

To be able to effectively lead your team, you must be focused on the process and recognize and release the external factors, the mental bricks that you cannot control that are keeping you from performing at your best.

 **COACHING POINT: What are the mental bricks that you need to let go of to effectively lead your team? What distractions have a tendency to deplete your energy and weigh you down?**

_____

_____

_____

8:00 SUMMARY

Live your life and lead your team 200 feet at a time.

Destination is the disease; journey is the reward.

Be into the process and not the outcome. You will experience a great outcome by working a great process.

Focus on "what is," not "what if," "What is" is what you can control.

Be into your performance, not just in.

W.I.N. = What's Important Now.

The future is just a bunch of what-you-do-right-nows strung together.

Don't count the days; make the days count.

Release your bricks.

8:00 APPLICATION

What are 5 key points you can apply to yourself and your team from this chapter?

1) _____

2) _____

3) _____

4) _____

5) _____

9:00

PURSUIT OF EXCELLENCE:
You vs. Yesterday

> *"The only easy day was yesterday."*
>
> **U.S. NAVY SEALs**

> *"The quality of a person's life is in direct proportion to their commitment to excellence, regardless of their chosen field."*
>
> **Vince Lombardi**
> **NFL Football Coach**

My grandfather and I were walking to Space Mountain at Disney World when he stopped and asked if I had seen the penny on the ground that I just stepped over. I had seen it but it didn't seem that important; after all, we were at Disney World and stopping to pick up a penny would have been a waste of time. Or so I thought.

PICKING UP PENNIES

He stopped me dead in my tracks and told me that picking up pennies would make me rich. I thought to myself, "I could spend my entire life picking up pennies and never become wealthy." Then, what he said changed my life – the "ah-ha" moment that helped me to begin to pursue excellence.

He said that picking up the penny had no bearing on monetary value; rather, it was the habit of picking up the penny - the habit of doing what others don't have time to do, are too busy to do, just don't want to do or don't think it is important enough to do. Every time you see a penny and you bend over and pick it up, you are reinforcing the skill of doing what other people don't want to do. Having the ability, which everyone does, of doing things that others don't want to do is as simple as picking up pennies.

Next time you see a penny on the ground, discipline yourself to pick it up. Be reminded that pursuing excellence and being successful are about doing what others are not willing to do. Excellence and success are uncommon, therefore not to be enjoyed by the common man.

FOCUS ON BEING BEST VERSION OF YOU

"Today you are You, that is truer than true. There is no one alive who is Youer than You!" – Dr. Seuss

Leaders hold themselves to higher standards of excellence. Excellence is being at your best when it means the most, both inside and outside your sport. It is focusing on the six inches between your ears so you can be in control of the six feet below them. It is not how good you are compared to other people; it is how good you are compared to how good you could be.

Many people think that they need to be better than the next person to be labeled as a success. Don't focus on others' achievements if you want to be successful because you may never add up to that person you are competing with. You have control of your own performance and being the best you can be. You don't have control over someone else, so strive to be the best YOU can possibly be.

John Wooden had this to say about excellence and being successful:

> *Don't try to be better than someone else. Always try to be the best you can be. Success is a peace of mind that is the direct result of self-satisfaction in knowing you did your best to become the best you are capable of becoming. Each one of us has a different mix of talents and a distinctive set of circumstances. In this context, each of us can learn to make the best effort we are capable of making, which may include changing some of our circumstances, if possible. If we refrain from comparing ourselves to others and stay off other people's ladders of success, we will have peace of mind.*

10 TRAITS OF THE BEST OF THE BEST

1. The best know what they truly want.

2. The best want it more.

3. The best are always striving to get better.

4. The best do ordinary things with extraordinary effort and attention to detail.

5. The best are mentally tougher.

6. The best overcome their fear.

7. The best seize the moment.

8. The best tap into a greater moment than themselves.

9. The best leave a legacy.

10. The best make everyone around them better.

THE PROBLEM WITH AVERAGE

Success is largely about discovering a winning formula and implementing the system that facilitates excellence.

Average people and average organizations are the best of the worst and the worst of the best. Do not settle for average; strive for excellence. It has been said that it is the start that stops most people. You don't have to be great to start, but to be great you have to get started. So why wait any longer? Get started, RIGHT NOW.

DECISION SHAPES DESTINY

Everything that happens in your life began with a decision. It is in your moments of decision that destiny is shaped. It is said that you are the product of the five people with whom you spend the most time. Show me your friends and I'll show you your future. Surround yourself with people who will make you better in every aspect of your life. If you surround yourself with those devoted to excellence, your chances of achieving it will drastically improve. When you invest your time properly to a winning system in striving for excellence, success will take care of itself.

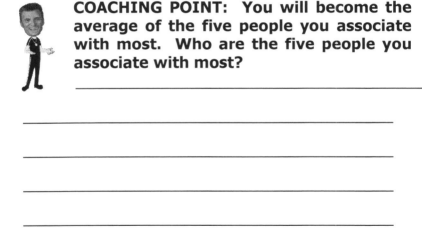

COACHING POINT: You will become the average of the five people you associate with most. Who are the five people you associate with most?

_____

_____

_____

_____

WHEN HAVE YOU SUCCEEDED?

When do you know that you have succeeded? When asking yourself this question, forget what others think. They don't know. What others perceive deals with your reputation. Reputations don't determine success, and neither do awards or accolades. Winning seems so important, but it is actually irrelevant in the journey to becoming successful.

Having attempted to give your all is what matters – and you are the only one who really knows the truth about your own efforts and performances. Did you do your best at this point of your life? Did you leave all you had in order to give on the field, in the classroom, at the office and in the trenches? If you did, then you are a success.

> *"Ultimate effort is ultimate victory."*
>
> **Keith Jardine**
> **Former UFC Fighter**

Being successful at one point doesn't necessarily make us a success at every point – and it doesn't mean that we reach the pinnacle of the mountain of excellence. We must learn to give our all in one success after another.

SUCCESS LEAVES CLUES

Here is some insight into achieving a successful career in everything you do: Success leaves clues. This concept will give insight into anything you do. If you want to be a millionaire, go hang out with people who are millionaires. If you hang out with people who are making $50,000 a year and you tell them you want to be a millionaire, what are they going to say? They are going to say that is impossible.

If you go hang out with millionaires, then you will gain insight and pick up clues as to how to make your first million. Imitation and adaptation to higher levels of competition will ultimately lead to performance improvement and success of your own. Surround yourself with people who are better than you. It may be tough on your ego but will be better for your team.

Most successful leaders were successful followers at some point. They learned how to be part of a team, put the needs of others ahead of their own, and work toward a goal bigger than themselves. In our hero-worshiping culture we tend to place the spotlight on the individual achievements of leaders and not pay much attention to how they cultivated those winning ways earlier in their career. Learn to be a good follower and you'll learn what it takes to be a good leader.

STUDY THE BEST

If you are a baseball pitcher and want to be the best you can be, go study the best pitchers in the game and see what has made them successful. If you want to be a better basketball player, watch LeBron James and Kevin Durant and mimic what they do in their training and conditioning.

Joe Torre, Hall of Fame Baseball manager and winner of four World Series titles with the New York Yankees, said this about success leaving clues:

> *One of the best ways to pick up leadership qualities is to draw from the leaders in your midst. Ask yourself who*

strikes you as being a great leader. Observe how they go about their business, try to put your finger on what makes them inspiring leaders.

PERFECTION IS UNATTAINABLE

In Gary Mack's book *Mind Gym*, he suggests an interesting experiment. Take someone with a strong fear of failure. Give that person some crumpled sheets of paper and ask the person to toss them into a small trash can from three different spots – directly over the can, fifteen feet away, and forty feet away. Studies have shown that those who fear failure will feel most anxious from the middle shot, fifteen feet away.

When standing directly over the basket, success is almost guaranteed. From forty feet away, there are no expectations. From fifteen feet, however, they feel that making the shot is very possible but know there is a chance they might fail. Where does this fear come from? Oftentimes, behind the fear of failure is trying to be perfect.

THE QUEST FOR PERFECTION

Perfection is unachievable; it is simply a philosophical idea. Why does the idea of being perfect control so much discussion in athletics? Perhaps it is because humans are obsessed by the thought of the unattainable. Perhaps we search for it because we are continuously unsatisfied with our flaws. Perhaps it is a combination of the two.

The quest for perfection serves as motivation for human improvement. It drives us forward, forces us to work harder, and makes us think we will perform better than in the past. It acts as the ever-present critic that challenges human beings to improve and achieve progress.

I once told someone I was a perfectionist. "Oh, yeah," the person said. "What have you been perfect at?" Gemologists can tell a real emerald from a fake one because the real ones are flawed.
Every leader has flaws, as no leader is perfect. Just because someone fails does not make him or her a failure. Look at fear as a natural part of growing and learning. Failure can be the greatest teacher you ever have - a better teacher than winning.

F.E.A.R. – FALSE EVIDENCE APPEARING REAL

Fear of failure, more than any single thing, keeps leaders in sports and in all avenues of life from realizing their full potential. Fear of failure prevents you from succeeding more than any opponent. Fear creates the conditions that keep athletes from performing at their best. It can severely restrict a person's ability to lead and can kill your performance. One of the paradoxes of sports is that fear of failure actually makes failure more likely.

TWO FEARS IN LIFE

There are only two fears in life. The two fears are that you are not good enough and that you will not be loved. The fear most coaches and athletes experience comes from fearing they are not good enough and having too much of their self-worth wrapped up in the outcome of their performance. You must constantly be building yourself up outside of your sport so that you can eliminate the fear of not being good enough in life should you fail at your sport.

Remember, sport is what you do, not who you are. If sport is who you are, check your priorities in life and work to create a better understanding of who you are off the field so you can turn the pressure you feel into pleasure.

PERFECTION IS A DOUBLE-EDGED SWORD

Perfection is a double-edged sword. On one hand, striving for perfection may be used to motivate people. But never achieving that desired perfection will certainly discourage some and act as the constant critic that zaps you of your confidence.

Instead of being perfect, focus on being just 1% better than you were yesterday. If you just strive to be 1% better every day, think how much better you will be in a week, a month, a year. This idea is known as the compound effect. Focus on getting a little bit better, 1% better, every single day; over a span of 365 days, that equates to major self-improvement. When you compete with others, you become bitter. When you compete with yourself, you become better.

University of Oregon jersey for 2013 Valero Alamo Bowl

Focus on being better than you were yesterday.

KAIZEN

Every day you are either getting better or getting worse. There is no staying the same. You are either growing or dying as a leader. "Kaizen" is a term the Japanese use to focus on constant daily learning and improvement over time. The concept of kaizen is used not only in sports but also in businesses around the world.

In the movie *Mr. Baseball*, where Tom Selleck plays New York Yankee power-hitting first baseman Jack Elliott, Jack becomes consumed with an extended slump and the club replaces him in the line-up with a younger player. Elliott's agent sends him to Japan, where he signs an enormous contract.

When Elliott reports to his new team, he is very arrogant. The former World Series MVP clashes with his no-nonsense, disciplinarian manager when the manager informs Jack that he has a "hole in his swing." Opposing pitchers notice this and do not offer him any fastballs. By the end of the movie Elliott, an arrogant know-it-all, learns how to be a better hitter and more complete player.

I noticed this firsthand while traveling to Japan with the a top group of baseball talent from the USA that the Japanese players focus on the process of knowing themselves and improving by small increments, every day. This concept applies directly to leadership. Leadership is developed daily, not overnight.

EXPENSIVE VS. INEXPENSIVE EXPERIENCE

There are two types of experience that you gather over your career. They are examples of experiences you are constantly gathering to help you learn, grow and take your performance to the next level. The two types are as follows:

Expensive: Comes from making your own mistakes and errors of judgment to learn life's many lessons. This is considered learning the hard way as you try to figure out everything on your own. It may cost you something, hence the name expensive.

Inexpensive: When you learn life's lessons from the expensive experience of others, learning from their past mistakes and successes.

Some experiences must be expensive, but a great deal of stress and frustration from expensive experience is preventable if you seek out mentors and listen and act on their advice.

There is much to be learned through the expensive experiences of historical figures, coaches, teachers or parents. A wise person learns from his mistakes, a wiser one learns from others' mistakes, but the wisest person learns from others' successes and failures. Except for what we garnered through personal experience, none of us knows anything that we didn't learn from someone else. Whatever the lesson, we saw somebody do it, we read about it, or we heard about it.

Abraham Lincoln could say a lot with just a few words. Lincoln said he never met a person from whom he did not learn something, although most of the time it was something not to do. There is a lot of truth in that.

Lincoln was always observing, alert to what was going on around him. He was constantly learning. When we aren't alert, we miss opportunities to improve ourselves. If we remain attentive, not only can we improve ourselves, but we can also learn not to repeat the errors of others. We should always watch for circumstances or situations that can help or harm us and be eager to learn from our encounters.

ATTENTION TO DETAIL

Leadership often places an emphasis on reaching goals and winning. What is overlooked is what it takes to get there – the day-to-day, minute-to-minute relevant details of how you do your job. Those under your leadership must be taught that little things make big things happen. There are no little things in the pursuit of excellence; they are all big things. This serves as a warning to those who want to shortcut the process. No relevant detail is too small to be done correctly.

Doing a thing nearly right and doing it exactly right is usually the difference between success and failure. Big things are accomplished only through the perfection of minor details. Races are won by fractions of a second. Championships are often won by a single point. This is the result of perfecting the relevant details along the way. Leave nothing to chance. That is the difference between good and great leaders, good and great teams - the perfection and execution of relevant details. Sloppiness breeds sloppiness.

Before you increase the intensity of your performance, you should be proficient in the fundamental skills necessary for such performance. There is no substitute for hard work. Most people have a tendency to look for shortcuts or at least for the easiest way to complete any given task.

If you only put forth minimum effort, you may get by in some situations, but in the long run you won't fully develop the talents that lie within you. There are no shortcuts on the path to success. Hard work beats talent when talent doesn't work hard.

As famous martial artist Bruce Lee said, "Don't fear the man who has practiced 10,000 kicks once; fear the man who has practiced one kick 10,000 times."

> *"The 'easy' button is available at Staples, but the 'effort' button is in your hands."*
>
> **Brett K. Basham**

PERFORMANCE EXCELLENCE

Performance excellence is about preparing more than other people are willing to and working smarter than other people think is necessary. It is a way of thinking and a way of acting. It is a quality of mind, a mentality that says that no matter how difficult things are, you are responsible and accountable for your thoughts, feelings and actions.

Performance excellence is staying positive in negative situations, and it is dealing with adversity in an optimistic way. People who excel at performance excellence look at competition and challenge as an opportunity vs. seeing the opportunity in every challenge.

They are motivated by a desire to succeed rather than by a fear of failure. They have a can-do attitude and a will to prepare to win.

3 STEPS FOR PERFORMANCE IMPROVEMENT

1. Awareness: Develop an awareness of what needs to change.

2. Strategy: Develop a strategy for change.

3. **Action:** Implement the strategy with an accountability partner, and assess yourself regularly so that the necessary performance change can occur.

Most people fall short of significant performance improvement because they either lack the awareness of what they need to change, do not formulate an effective strategy for change, fail to implement the strategy to bring about the necessary change, or have a YES partner instead of an accountability partner.

A YES partner is someone who tells you how great you are and tells you what you want to hear, not what you need to hear.

 COACHING POINT: List three people you know who pursue excellence every day and what they do that makes you say that.

1) _____

2) _____

3) _____

List the 3 most excellent teammates you have and what they do that makes you say that about them.

1) _____

2) _____

3) _____

What are some things that leaders who display excellence do in practice?

1) _____

2) _____

3) _____

What are some things that leaders who display excellence do in competition?

1) _____

2) _____

3) _____

What are some things that leaders who display excellence do in school?

1) _____

2) _____

3) _____

What are some things that leaders who display excellence do in the community?

1) _____

2) _____

3) _____

As a leader, what does excellence mean to you, and how can you demonstrate it to your team?

_____

_____

_____

9:00 SUMMARY

Focus on being the best version of you.

Success leaves clues.

Average people and average teams are the best of the worst and the worst of the best.

Perfection is unattainable.

F.E.A.R. stands for False Evidence Appearing Real.

Use the compound effect to be 1% better than you were yesterday.

Expensive vs. inexpensive are the two types of experience.

Leaders pay close attention to detail.

There are 3 steps for performance improvement: awareness, strategy, action.

9:00 APPLICATION

What are 5 key points you can apply to yourself and your team from this chapter?

1) _____

2) _____

3) _____

4) _____

5) _____

PART IV

MAKING THE PEOPLE AROUND YOU BETTER

10:00

CONFIDENCE:
A Choice and Action, Not a Feeling

> *"A good leader inspires others with confidence in him; a great leader inspires them with confidence in themselves."*
>
> ***Unknown***

The date was September 26, 1960, the day of the very first televised Presidential debate between Vice President Richard Nixon and Massachusetts Senator John F. Kennedy. Earlier in the day, Nixon seriously injured his knee while getting out of his car on the way to the event. Although he was in tremendous pain, Nixon refused stage makeup to mask his discomfort and profuse sweating.

He stood behind his podium favoring his injured leg. With his body leaning awkwardly to one side, Nixon appeared crooked and off balance; not a look or feel that inspires confidence in a future President. As 70 million U.S. viewers tuned in to watch Senator Kennedy and Vice President Nixon in this first televised Presidential debate, many of them noticed the stark contrast between the two. Nixon appeared with his hands hidden behind the podium, perspiring and clearly uncomfortable. Kennedy, in comparison, appeared calm, cool and collected. According to the poll of the radio audience, who only heard the candidates speak, Nixon won the debate by a landslide. In a similar poll of television viewers, Nixon lost by a landslide. John F. Kennedy ended up winning the Presidency in 1960.

Many experts still believe that if Nixon had really understood the impact of his body language, he may have paid closer attention to the image he was projecting and history might have turned out quite differently.

Although Nixon may not have lacked any confidence, he was perceived as unsure and not confident because of his body language, and it ultimately cause him a chance to be President of the United States....at that time.

CONFIDENCE IS CRITICAL

There is one particular component of leadership that is critically important; without it, leadership cannot exist. That component is confidence. Confidence is a choice. It is not boasting or swagger or an overt pretense of bravery. Confidence is not some bold or brash air of self-belief directed at others. Confidence is quiet: It's a natural expression of ability, expertise and self-regard.

FEELINGS ARE FALSE

Yes, confidence can be a feeling, but it is more of an action. Many people think they have to feel confident to act confident, but that isn't true. You don't have to feel confident to act confident, you don't have to feel great to act great, and you don't have to feel like a leader to lead.

One of the actions of confidence is having positive body language. In the example above, having negative body language one time lost the Presidency for one man. By showing positive body language, you will come across as having confidence, even if you don't at the time. Body language doesn't whisper; it screams!

ABC's OF CONFIDENCE

Remember the ABC's of confidence:

Always Behave Confidently. As Dr. Tom Hanson writes about in his book *Play Big,* you need to act big, breathe big and commit big. Actions change attitudes. Motions change emotions. Movement changes moods. Act confident and the feelings of confidence will follow.

Every athlete hears two competing voices. One is a negative critic and the other a positive coach. The one we listen to is a matter of choice.

FEEDING THE TWO WOLVES

A wise Indian chief with a background in sport psychology tells the story of the two wolves that live inside of each of us. One wolf is powerful and positive; the other is weak and negative. These two wolves go to battle inside of us each day. The one who wins the battle for your conscious mind is the one that you train. Are you training your positive wolf and the positive voice in your head, or are you training the negative wolf and the negative voice inside of your head?

Confidence is the fundamental basis from which leadership grows. When the leader lacks confidence, the followers lack commitment. Trying to teach leadership without first building confidence is like building a house on a foundation of sand. It may have a nice coat of paint, but it is ultimately shaky at best.

LEADERS MAKE DECISIONS

At the end of the day, leadership is about having the confidence to make tough decisions. If someone is afraid to make and commit to decisions, all of the communication and empowerment in the world won't make any difference. Not only does confidence allow you to make the tough decisions that people expect from a strong leader, but it's reassuring to your teammates. You can only delegate so many responsibilities. At some point, you must be confident enough to make the tough calls on your own.

Be confident in your decision-making, but also have the confidence to say, "I don't know, but let me find out and get back to you."

Your Time to Lead Is Now!

Sometimes a mistake that leaders make is thinking that they have to have all the answers and there is only one way. Leaders are always searching for the best way, and they are always growing from those experiences. As a leader, if you aren't growing, you're dying.

KNOWING VS. FINDING OUT WHAT TO DO

To have confidence in yourself isn't always being right. Confidence isn't always knowing exactly what to do. It is about discovering the best course of action to take. Confidence is finding out what my team needs to help them get over the hurdle or get them to where they need to be.

Confidence is not always knowing if you have the answer. It is knowing how to find the right answer by having self-confidence to ask the people in the organization or team what they need. You might not know as a leader - you don't always know what people need. You do have to know the process of finding out what they need. Leadership is not about having all the answers and it's not always about being right.

COACHING POINT: Think back to the times when you were the most confident. What did that feel like? What did it look like with your body language? What was your energy like? Write down as much as you can remember about what it was like to be your most confident self.

www.BrianCain.com   185

_____

_____

_____

_____

_____

What other aspects of your life do you need to work on to become a more confident leader?

_____

_____

_____

HUMILITY

Humility is also a critical part of leadership and is often overlooked as a part of confidence. As a leader, you must have the balance of humility and confidence.

Humility allows you to know that you don't have all the answers and that you must continue to get better. Confidence allows you to compete and make decisions you must make as a leader and trust that you are making the correct decisions.

Humility can be a tough pill to swallow, but it is reality. As a leader, you must have confidence in your own ability and, more importantly, in your team. But often trouble comes when that confidence turns into arrogance. With humility, you are reminded of where you came from and that the future is not guaranteed.

Humility is not about demeaning yourself, shrugging off your accomplishments, or downplaying yourself in any way. Humility means that you know where you are, where you've been, and what you have accomplished to get where you are. Humility is also knowing that you are going somewhere and that where you are is a stop on the journey - a stop only made because of the help and support of others.

With that knowledge, you can get out of your own way and focus on others with the confidence that you can lead, inspire and guide people - that you can help them to do and become more than their own vision for themselves. A good leader inspires people to have confidence in the leader. A great leader inspires people to have confidence in themselves.

3 KEYS TO CONFIDENCE

1. Physiology: When talking about physiology, two words that my mentor Dr. Ken Ravizza would always say come to mind: GET BIG. Carry yourself big and move fast. Dr. David Schwartz talks about big body language in his book *The Magic of Thinking Big*. He writes that successful leaders walk at a rate 25% faster than others.

Start walking faster today and see what that does for your physiology and getting big. Body language doesn't whisper; it screams. It is every bit as important as the words you say and how you say them combined.

2. Focus: Make sure you focus on only those aspects of your performance that you can control and let go of the uncontrollable aspects. Controlling the controllable aspects of your life and sport is an essential ingredient in focus.

3. Self-Talk: How are you talking to yourself? Are you telling yourself that you can or you can't? Are you telling yourself what you want to do instead of what you want to avoid? If you focus on positive self-talk, it will allow you to perform the GET BIG and focus keys to confidence.

ADVERTISE TO YOURSELF

Advertise to yourself the mentality and the goals that you want. McDonald's Theory says that most people think they can make a hamburger better than McDonald's does. But McDonald's makes billions of dollars selling hamburgers. Why? Because they do it every single day, multiple times a day. They take action and advertise to the people about the millions of people that enjoy their hamburgers every day. They may not be the best hamburgers, but people still buy and eat them.

THE 10 DEADLY WORDS

There are ten deadly words that will crush your performance if you say them or believe them. If you're trying to be excellent, if you're trying to get to the top of your field, then paying attention to these ten deadly words will sabotage your career: "What will other people say? What will other people think?"

What other people say and think is outside of your control. Therefore, it doesn't matter what people say or think. In your pursuit of excellence, people are going to try to pull you down and talk about you because you are striving to become better than they are - and that makes them feel insecure. When you face critics, remember to tune them out and focus only on being the best you can be.

Get used to looking at yourself in the mirror, questioning your commitment and answering in the affirmative.

Every night when your head hits the pillow, that's the person you will answer to.

Other people are going to tell you that you can't do it. Listening to these people and internalizing their negative beliefs is counterproductive to achieving your goals. People can only hurt your feelings in areas where you already feel insecure.

Author C. S. Lewis said, "By mixing a little truth with it, they make their lies much stronger."

Here's a **lie:** Your worth as a person depends on what another person says, does or thinks about you.

Do not let broken people tell you how broken you are. Don't worry about what people think of you; focus on what is right vs. what is wrong. Focus on being respected rather than liked. Remember, when a man wants to lead the orchestra, he must turn his back to the crowd.

It is not the critic who counts; not the man who points out how the strong man stumbles, or where the doer of deeds could have done them better. The credit belongs to the man who is actually in the arena, whose face is marred by dust and sweat and blood; who strives valiantly; who errs, who comes short again and again, because there is no effort without error and shortcoming; but who does actually strive to do the deeds; who knows great enthusiasms, the great devotions; who spends himself in a worthy cause; who at the best knows in the end the triumph of high achievement, and who at the worst, if he fails, at least fails while daring greatly, so that his place shall never be with those cold and timid souls who neither know victory nor defeat.

President Theodore Roosevelt

If you live or lead like you are trying to be the smartest, prettiest or most athletic, you will never feel like enough. There will always be someone or something else you think is better. If your confidence is based on the subjective opinion of others vs. living your values, you will never be truly confident.

Hall of Fame baseball player Ozzie Smith said, "Show me a guy who is afraid of looking bad and I can beat him every time."

BELIEF –
THE GIFT THAT KEEPS ON GIVING

One of the greatest gifts you can give to your followers is telling and showing them that you believe in them and what they are doing. You should believe in them even when they fail or when they haven't been the best friend, teammate or player they could have been. Oftentimes, as a coach or team leader, you will criticize and get angry with your followers when they commit a wrong. That is OK; they need to be held accountable. The fault is not being there to pick them up off the ground and reinforcing the belief in them that you know you have. The best leaders will tell you, even when you are at your worst, that you are going to make it and that they believe in you. The mark of a great leader is believing in people, even when they are at their worst, because you know they have success inside of them.

Belief is defined as an acceptance that a statement is true or that something exists - trust, faith or confidence in someone or something. You must believe in yourself and who you are as a person. This is the only way to get others to believe in you. There are three sources of belief that athletes use to build and maintain their confidence:

1. Strengths: The strengths you possess are a great way to build confidence. Knowing what you do well, both personally and as a team, will allow you and your group to be able to accomplish goals in practices and games. Acknowledge your flaws and the flaws of your

teammates, and work to improve in those areas. However, make sure you rely on your strengths for belief in yourself and your team.

2. Previous Accomplishments: You may want to refer back to expensive and inexpensive experience. The experiences you have accrued over the span of your life, whether positive or negative, will help in your belief. If it was a positive experience, rely on that when you are in a game situation and the pressure is on. If it was negative, remember what went wrong and what you should have done to correct it. That will allow for a more positive result this time around. Experience tells you what to do; belief allows you to do it.

3. Praise from others: Belief can be inspired by thoughts from others. Whether it is praise from coaches, teammates, parents, etc., it is nice to hear that your superiors and peers are acknowledging your practice or play in games. However, be cautious when it comes to praise from others. Sure, you will be praised when positive moments happen, but you can't control how people will react when negatives occur.

> *As I say to the professional athletes I work with, don't bother reading the paper. If you believe it when it is going good and they are kissing your butt, you will believe it when you are going bad and they are kicking it.*

You may not be around people that give praise very much, so you must learn that belief comes from within. It's nice to have your beliefs affirmed by others, but if you don't have belief in yourself, none of that matters.

PREPARATION

Most people think success is luck, and they keep trying to win the lottery of life. Success is really the result of planning and execution. It happens where preparation and opportunity meet and execution occurs.

When we are as prepared as we know how to be and we know that we have the tools to handle most of the unknowns that might come our way, we can go into a practice, a game, a class, a show or any other venue with confidence. There is no more important ingredient to an athlete's success than quality preparation.

> *"The separation is in preparation."*
>
> ***Russell Wilson***
> ***Quarterback***
> ***Seattle Seahawks***
> ***Super Bowl Champion***

It is an essential key to having confidence - learning how to properly prepare to be at your best when it is needed the most.

John Wooden said, "Failing to prepare is preparing to fail." If we don't invest time preparing, we will most assuredly spend time repairing. Practice doesn't make perfect; practice makes permanent. Over-prepare so you don't underperform.

POISE

Most people think of poise with words such as calm and self-esteem. Poise is just "being you."

You don't have to try to be something you're not, and you don't have to live up to others' expectations of what they think you should be. Therefore, when you are being yourself, you will have a greater likelihood of performing within your own level of capability. If you possess poise, other people's thoughts will be of no concern to you. Outside influences won't change who you are or what you try to be. You'll never try to be anything other than who you are. As long as you are at ease with yourself, you will be able to function near your own ability.

> "If you think you are beaten, you are;
> If you think you dare not, you don't.
> If you'd like to win, but think you can't,
> It's almost a cinch you won't.
>
> "If you think you'll lose, you've lost,
> For out in the world we find
> Success being with a fellow's will;
> It's all in the state of mind.
>
> "If you think you're outclassed, you are:
> You've got to think high to rise.
> You've got to be sure of yourself before
> You can ever win a prize.
>
> "Life's battles don't always go
> To the stronger or faster man,
> But soon or late the man who wins
> Is the one who thinks he can."
>
> Walter D. Wintle

COACHING POINT: What have you done in your preparation that allows you to be confident as a leader?

_____

_____

What are your strengths as a leader?

_____

_____

What previous accomplishments will allow you to perform at your best and to lead successfully?

_____

_____

Who are some people who have supported you, and what types of praise have they given you to help you perform and be a better leader?

_____

_____

10:00 SUMMARY

ABC's of confidence: Always Behave Confidently.
As a leader you must have the balance of humility and confidence.

Confidence is not always knowing if you have the answer. It is knowing how to find the right answer by having self-confidence to ask the people in the organization or team what they need.

3 keys to confidence: Physiology, Focus, Self-Talk

Your worth as a person does not depend on what another person says, does or thinks about you.

The separation is in preparation.

You don't have to try to be something you're not, and you don't have to live up to others' expectations of what they think you should be.

10:00 APPLICATION

What are 5 key points you can apply to yourself and your team from this chapter?

1) _____

2) _____

3) _____

4) _____

5) _____

11:00

ABILITY TO INSPIRE
AND MOTIVATE

Look Inside, See What You Find

> *"Leadership is not about titles, positions, or flowcharts. It is about one life influencing another."*
>
> **John Maxwell**
> **Leadership Expert**

Simple Truths produced a tremendous motivational and leadership video and program called *212*.

At 211 degrees, water is hot. At 212 degrees, it boils. And with boiling water comes steam, which can power a locomotive. One extra degree makes all the difference. The one extra degree of effort, in sports and in life, separates the good from the great!

The average margin of victory for the last 25 years of all PGA Golf Majors combined was less than three strokes. The margin of victory between an Olympic gold medal and no medal at all is very small. At the Indy 500, the average margin of victory the past 10 years has been 1.54 seconds. On average, the winner took home $1.2 million while second place received $621,000 - which is less than half of the winner!
It's your life, it's your team. It's time to turn up the heat! To get what we've never had, we must do what we've never done. You are now aware. You now have a target for everything you do.

"68"

There are certain things that Jaromir Jagr is known for. First is his reputation as one of the NHL's all-time greats. Jagr used his skills to help guide his teams to the highest achievements, picking up personal accolades along the way that will undoubtedly land him in the Hockey Hall of Fame. His resume includes winning an Olympic gold medal playing for the Czech Republic in 1998, a pair of Stanley Cups with the Pittsburgh Penguins in 1991 and 1992, and five NHL scoring titles.

However, there is more to Jagr's story than just his ability on the ice. Jagr has worn the number 68 ever since beginning his NHL career in 1990 at the age of 18. Even though 68 is a strange number to pick, Jagr uses that number as motivation.

In 1968, the Soviet army invaded the home country of Jagr's family, Czechoslovakia. The Prague Spring, as it was called, was the ultimately unsuccessful Czechoslovakian rebellion against the Soviet Union. Jagr's grandfather, also named Jaromir, was imprisoned during the rebellion for refusing to work on his own farm for free after it was confiscated by Soviet troops. He died in prison. Even though Jagr was not born until four years after his grandfather's death, he learned about his grandfather's courage through other family members.

While much has changed, Jagr has kept the spirit of "68" on the back of his jersey on every team he has played for since he ascended to hockey superstardom

24 years ago. The number 68 was Jaromir Jagr's motivation; it is what kept him going.

Everyone has something that motivates and pushes them when they don't want to be pushed. For Jagr, it was the thought of honoring his late grandfather for the courageous struggle he went through in standing up for what he believed in. What is your 68? What keeps you motivated on a daily basis to be the most successful athlete, coach, person and/or leader you can be?

Motivation could be the desire to succeed or the need to avoid pain and failure. What we associate with pleasure we pursue, while what we associate with pain we try to avoid at all costs.

So what motivates people? Take a moment and link the definition of leadership (influence) with the responsibility of leadership (development of others). How do we influence others? How do we truly motivate and develop them? We do it through encouragement and belief in them. People tend to become what the most important people in their lives think they will become.

TAKE THE AIR OUT

Imagine if all of the air got sucked out of where you are right now; what would happen to your interest in this book? You wouldn't care about the book. You wouldn't care about anything except getting air, and survival would be your only motivation. Now imagine that the air is let back in. Since you have air, it doesn't motivate you. This is one of the greatest perceptions in human motivation: Satisfied needs do not motivate. It's only unsatisfied needs that motivate. It is the same with athletics.

Everyone wants to win a state or national championship in their sport, which is what motivates and drives them. In other words, they have to have something to satisfy their needs. But once that win happens, teams tend to become complacent and they lose their motivation. That is why it is so hard to repeat as a champion in sports. It is human nature to be complacent once our needs are satisfied. Inspire and motivate yourself and your teammates to make the impossible possible. Without inspiration, the best powers of the mind remain dormant. There is a fuel in us which needs to be ignited with sparks. Remember, the dream is free, but the hustle is sold separately.

4 FACTORS OF MOTIVATION

1. Significant contributions: People want to join a group or pursue a cause that will have a lasting impact. They need to see that what they are doing is not wasted effort but is making a contribution. Motivation comes not by activity alone, but by the desire to reach the end result.

2. Goal participation: Being a part of the goal-setting process is motivating, and it allows people to feel needed. They like to feel they are making a difference. Goal participation builds team spirit, enhances morale and helps everyone feel important.

3. Positive dissatisfaction: Dissatisfied people are highly motivated people, for they see the need for immediate change. They know something is wrong and often know what needs to be done.

Dissatisfaction can inspire change or it can lead to a critical spirit. It can lead to apathy or stir one to change. The key is harnessing this energy toward effective change.

4. Clear expectations: People are motivated when they know exactly what they are to do and have the confidence that they can do it successfully. No one wants to jump into a task that is vague or a job with an uncertain description. People perform better when they have some control over their work and their time.

TAKE A LOOK INSIDE, SEE WHAT YOU FIND

On May 6, 1954, Roger Bannister, a British medical student and avid runner, did the previously unimaginable. From the start of archiving world records and modern time-keeping track events, no one had been able to break the seemingly impossible task of running a sub-four-minute mile.

People had been trying to achieve it since the days of the ancient Greeks. Greek officials had tried the use of lions as well. They would release the lions in hopes that the runners would be able to outrun them and break the barrier in the process. Eventually, it was proclaimed that this feat was impossible. Wind resistance was too strong, human bone structure won't allow it, and inadequate lung power were just a few of the excuses that scientists had come up with.

Bannister's story demonstrates the prophecy of thought and the power that lies within us.

Bannister was a very successful track athlete, competing in the mile and 1500-meter events and drawing national attention. However, he shunned the 1948 Olympic Games in London to concentrate on his medical studies and training. His fourth place finish in the 1500-meter race at the 1952 Olympics in Helsinki, the result of a last-minute schedule change compromising his preparation routines, drew further scrutiny for his unusual training regimen.

After the media publicized his Olympic performance as failure, Bannister committed to redeem himself by striving to break the impossible four-minute mile barrier. He was committed to his training and loyal to the process that would get him there, instead of shortchanging himself like he did in 1952. He was convinced that as long as he continued to see gradual improvements in his times, he would maintain his own training regimen.

May 6, 1954, changed the sports world forever. In a meet between the British Amateur Athletic Association and Oxford University at the Iffley Road Track in Oxford, England, running mates set the pace for Bannister's first three laps. During the fourth and final lap,

Bannister "kicked it into high gear" and finished in under one minute. Upon breaking the tape at the finish line, he collapsed into the arms of the gathered crowd. The race announcer confirmed what many in the crowd already knew: 3:59.4. Roger Bannister had made history!

This example is physical evidence that there is success deep inside all of us. We choose self-limiting barriers because we listen to others around us saying certain achievements are impossible. The four-minute mile was once thought to be impossible. Then one man proved everyone wrong - the doctors and trainers, and the athletes and people before him who had tried and failed. Once the self-limiting barrier had been broken, people started to believe.

The most amazing part of the Roger Bannister story is that the year after Bannister accomplished the feat, 37 runners succeeded in running a sub-four-minute mile.

The year after that, 300 runners did it. There were no breakthroughs in training or changes in human anatomy. The only breakthrough that happened was one man and his belief to accomplish a task. By looking inside himself and finding the will to accomplish a task, Bannister changed the world. He inspired people to get moving and change their attitudes. You can always do more than you think you can. There is always more inside of you if you're willing to work hard enough to bring it out.

YOU + MOTIVATION = SUCCESS

Leaders get people moving. They inspire and motivate. They take people and teams to places they have never been before. Rarely will players go the extra mile unless they feel respected, empowered and motivated. Leaders inspire those they lead to take a look inside of themselves and see what they find. When you do that and ask yourself why you do what you do or what your purpose is, you can often find a motivation that can't be created by an outside source. Take a look inside of yourself. When you search within yourself, you learn that all the answers to life's questions are hidden inside you.

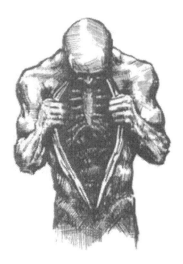

Once you get your teammates to look inside themselves and find that untapped potential that is inside of them, you create a motivated team. When you can shift from getting frustrated to getting fascinated, and can do that by taking a look at what you can learn from each and every opportunity, you will truly be successful. What lies behind us and what lies before us are tiny matters compared to what lies within us.

FEDEX LOGO CHANGES LIVES

Have you seen the FedEx logo before?

Have you seen the arrow between the E and the X? What about the spoon in the curve of the first E? This FedEx logo is the perfect metaphor for changing your perspective, for reaching deep down inside of you for something that has been hidden there for a long time. A logo you have seen a million times suddenly transforms into something you have never seen or never paid attention to.

That's what leaders do; they inspire others to find whatever is inside themselves that they may have never been able to see before. Leaders inspire others to see themselves as they have never seen themselves before.

As a leader, getting teammates to change their perspective is essential to development. Leaders get people moving. They inspire and motivate. They take people and organizations to places they have never been before. Rarely will players go the extra mile unless they feel valued, empowered, and motivated. If you aren't inspired, don't expect your team to be.

COMMITMENT

"There are only two options regarding commitment. You are either IN or you're OUT. There is no such thing as life in between." – Pat Riley, former NBA Champion Coach and current President of the Miami Heat.

In John Maxwell's book *The 21 Indispensable Qualities of a Leader*, he writes that leaders need to not only be committed but also embrace commitment. There has never been a leader who lacked commitment to the cause. Commitment means staying loyal to what you said you were going to do long after the mood you said it in has left you. True commitment inspires and motivates those you lead. They will believe in you only if you believe in yourself and what you are trying to do. People will ultimately be sold on the leader's commitment, then the vision. People don't care how much you know, until they know how much you care. Let's look at three observations from John Maxwell, the world's leading authority on leadership:

1. Commitment starts in the heart: The winning horse in the Kentucky Derby runs out of oxygen after the first mile of the race. It finishes the race based on heart. If you want to capture the hearts of the people you lead, look into your own heart first and see how committed you are.

2. Commitment is tested by action: You must walk the walk when it comes to commitment. There is no sense in talking about being committed while your actions

suggest otherwise. Nothing is easier than saying words. Nothing is harder than living them.

3. Commitment opens the door to achievement: You will face adversity as a leader. There will be times when your commitment is the only thing that compels you to keep moving forward.

GOAL SETTING

The best way to motivate yourself and others around you is to measure progress toward a specific goal. Simply believing that you will give your best without specific measurement of performance is unrealistic. Focus on process goals instead of outcome goals. Outcome goals often center on destinations such as becoming state champions or making an All-American team, which are important, but they shouldn't be set ahead of process goals. The reasoning for this is that we don't have goals that concentrate on control over outcome. Focus on goals you can control. Goals improve performance. They clarify expectations and help increase self-confidence by seeing yourself get better.

SMART GOALS

The best goals are written with the SMART method in mind:
S – Specific: They need to be as detailed as possible. Give yourself specific goals that are centered on your area of sport.

M – Measurable: Can we set numerical targets to track progress and results?

A – Attainable: Is it possible to get the results you want? The goal is reachable and is in your control.

R – Realistic: What talents are required, how do we get them, who must we work with to reach them, and what problems will we face? It is fully believable.

T – Time-Bound: There is a specific deadline. A goal is a dream with a timeline; every goal needs a target date for completion.

Focus on the process instead of the outcome - the goals that you have control over instead of ones where you have no control. Don't dwell on issues that keep you up at night; set goals according to what motivates you to get up in the morning. Once you set a goal, there are three key steps to making that goal come to fruition, according to top sales trainer Frank Somma:

3 STEPS FOR GOAL ATTAINMENT

1. Make a commitment: There is a big difference between a promise and a commitment. Losers make promises; winners keep commitments. A promise is something that you might keep, if you feel like it. A commitment is rock solid; it will get done.

Examples of a commitment could be: "I am going to study for three hours tonight," "I am going to run five miles today," "I am going to..."

2. Make it public: Tell everyone what you are going to do. By telling everyone, you will have the social pressure. It will serve as extra motivation to not look foolish by backing out of a commitment.

3. Make it happen: DO IT! Make the commitment come to life.

VISION BOARDS

It is essential that you use strategies to motivate and inspire action and accomplishment every day. By using a vision board, you will be surrounded with images that will inspire the achievement of greatness. Remember, THOUGHTS BECOME THINGS and what is thought about is brought about. Our actions move in the direction of our most dominant thoughts. You are today where your thoughts have brought you; you will be tomorrow where your thoughts take you. Visualize consistent and successful performance. We respond to what we see. Imagine only brushing your teeth once a week. You cannot brush your teeth once a week and expect them to look good or feel good. You must do a little a lot and brush them each day. You should absorb some form of inspiration daily to motivate you in your preparation and performance.

One of the best motivational exercises you can do as a leader and as a team to help with inspiration and motivation is to create a vision board. A vision board is simply a collage of your goals and what you desire to accomplish. This is a great team-building and team-focusing exercise. When you create a visual image of what it is you want to accomplish, you increase your chances of accomplishing that goal by 35%.

You will never outperform your self-image. Making a vision board will inspire you to accomplish your goals. Place it where you can see it every day. This will keep your goals in front of you and motivate you to achieve them.

THERMOSTAT OR THERMOMETER

When it comes to leadership, are you a thermostat or a thermometer? A thermometer reflects the temperature of the environment. It simply reacts to what's happening around it. It is passive. It records the temperature but can do nothing to change the environment. If the temperature is hot, it tells you that it's hot. If it's cold, the thermometer reflects that reality as well. It's a dumb instrument in the sense that it does not contain intelligent, multipurpose functionality. It has one purpose and one purpose only: to read the temperature and relay that to you. It is 100% responsive to the environment, has no personal power and acts only on the outside factors.

A thermostat is an active instrument and regulates the environment. It sets the desired temperature of the room and actively works to maintain it within a given range. If the temperature rises above the goal, the thermostat signals the air conditioner to crank up and cool the room down. If the temperature falls below the goal, the thermostat causes the heater to turn on in order to warm the room up. The thermostat is intelligent in the sense that it's always monitoring the environment, and if the temperature gets too hot or cold, it decides what to do to correct the situation. It effects change in order to create a climate.

Thermometer leaders react to their surroundings. When the tension gets high and people are on edge, these leaders are often seen losing their cool. They become irritable, harsh, demanding, critical, impatient, and maybe even lose their temper and yell or curse. Thermometer leadership doesn't inspire trust and commitment with people; rather, it erodes trust and commitment.

Thermostat leaders, however, constantly have a pulse on the morale, productivity, stress level and environmental conditions of their team. When the temperature gets hot because the team is under pressure of a heavy workload, resources are scarce or pending deadlines are causing stress, they cool things off by acting as the calming influence with the team. They take time to listen to the concerns of their team members and provide the necessary direction and support needed to help the team achieve its goals. Thermostat leaders also ease pressure on their team by mixing in some lighthearted fun at opportune times.

Likewise, when work is slow and people are prone to just go through the motions, thermostat leaders get their teams refocused on the vision, purpose and goals of the team. Thermostat leaders are actively monitoring the environment of their teams; they know when the team needs to be challenged with new goals and priorities, or when they just need a friendly kick in the pants to stay focused on the process.

Thermostat leaders build trust and confidence with their followers, whereas thermometer leaders erode trust. When times get wild and crazy, people want their leaders to react with calm, focused and determined leadership. They want them to set the tone for how the team should react during tough times and navigate the rough seas ahead.

That's a tough challenge for leaders since they are team members themselves and are subject to the same, and oftentimes more and different, stressors of those experienced by the team.

 **COACHING POINT: Are you a thermometer or thermostat leader?**

When was the last time that you attempted something new and it did not work out?

_____

_____

How did that failure affect you?

_____

_____

Describe an event in your life when fear was present but you did what you needed to do anyway in spite of the fear.

_____

_____

Describe a time in your life when a situation forced you take a look inside of yourself and dig deeper than you knew you could dig.   What did you discover about yourself and your ability to motivate?

_____

_____

11:00 SUMMARY

At 211° water is hot. At 212° water boils, making steam. Steam can power a locomotive.

Satisfied needs do not motivate.

You + Motivation = Success.

Leaders get people moving. They inspire and motivate.

There are only two options in commitment: You're either IN or OUT.

Set SMART goals for yourself and your team.

3 steps for goal attainment:
1. Make a commitment.
2. Make it public.
3. Make it happen.

Be a thermostat, not a thermometer.

11:00 APPLICATION

What are 5 key points you can apply to yourself and your team from this chapter?

1) _____

2) _____

3) _____

4) _____

5) _____

12:00

SELFLESSNESS:
It's about WE, not Me

> *"The secret to success is good leadership, and good leadership is all about making the lives of your team members better."*
>
> **Tony Dungy**

In the final battle scene from the World War II film *Saving Private Ryan*, mortally wounded Captain John H. Miller whispers his last words into Private James Ryan's ears: "Earn this," he says between short breaths before he slumps his head, his task complete.

His task was to find Private Ryan and bring him home, a mission of mercy and selflessness planned to give his mother some solace after she hears that three of her four sons died on the field. Miller and his specially picked squad end up completing their task, at the cost of most of their own lives; yet they successfully complete their mission, to bring Private Ryan home alive.

In the final minutes of the movie, after Miller's passionate imperative to "Earn this," the camera cuts to an elderly James Ryan (played by Matt Damon) standing over Miller's grave. With tears in his eyes, Ryan speaks to the departed Miller at his grave: "Every day I think about what you said to me that day on the bridge; I've tried to live my life the best that I could. I hope that that was enough. I hope that, at least in your eyes, I earned what you did for me."

What Miller did to save the life of another soldier so he could get back to see his mother was selfless. He put someone else's life in front of his and helped a young man achieve his goal, while dying in the process. His act was the true definition of selflessness; genuine consideration for others, an eagerness to sacrifice personal interests of glory for the welfare of all. You are a true success when you help others be successful. A life not lived for others is not a life at all.

MAKING THE CALL

On June 28, 2005, deep behind enemy lines in the Hindu Kush Mountains of Afghanistan, a four-man Navy SEAL team was conducting an intelligence and reconnaissance mission at the challenging altitude of 10,000 feet. The SEALs were Lieutenant Michael Murphy, Gunner's Mate 2nd Class Danny Dietz, Sonar Technician 2nd Class Matthew Axelson, and Hospital Corpsman 2nd Class Marcus Luttrell. They had the vital task of scouting Ahmad Shah – a Taliban loyalist who killed a group of American soldiers in previous weeks and grew up in the adjacent mountains just to the south.

Under the assumed name Muhammad Ismail, Shah led a guerrilla group known to locals as the "Mountain Tigers" that had aligned with the Taliban and other militant groups close to the Pakistani border. The SEAL mission was compromised when the team was spotted by local goat herders, who likely reported the team's presence and location to Shah and his followers.

A fierce firefight erupted between the four SEALs and a much larger enemy force of militia. The enemy had the SEALs outnumbered and also had terrain advantage. They launched a well-organized, three-sided attack on the SEALs. The firefight continued relentlessly as the overwhelming militia forced the team deeper into a ravine.

Trying to reach safety, the four men, each now wounded, began bounding down the mountain's steep sides, making leaps of 20 to 30 feet. Approximately 45 minutes into the fight, pinned down by overwhelming forces, Dietz sought open air to place a distress call back to the base. Before he could make the call, he was shot in the hand, shattering his thumb.

Despite the intensity of the firefight and suffering grave gunshot wounds himself, Murphy risked his own life to save the lives of his teammates. Murphy, intent on making contact with headquarters, realized it was impossible in the extreme terrain where they were fighting. Unhesitatingly and with complete disregard for his own life he moved into the open, where he gained a better position to transmit a call to get help for his men.

Moving away from the protective mountain rocks, he knowingly exposed himself to increased enemy gunfire. This deliberate and heroic act deprived him of cover and made him a target for the enemy. While continuing to be fired upon, Murphy made contact with the SOF Quick Reaction Force at Bagram Air Base and requested assistance. He calmly provided his unit's location and the size of the enemy force while requesting immediate support for his team.

At one point he was shot in the back, causing him to drop the transmitter. Murphy picked it up, completed the call and continued firing at the enemy, who was closing in. At the end of his radio transmission for help, despite his severe wounds and dire situation, Murphy – ever the officer and gentleman – said, "Thank you."

Lieutenant Michael Murphy illustrated what servant leadership is all about. He made the ultimate sacrifice for the rest of his team. Couldn't he have commanded another to do what he wanted? Surely he wasn't the only member of the team capable of making that call.

IT'S ABOUT WE, NOT ME

This is the first question a leader should ask: "How can I help make those around me more successful?" It is about setting up people you lead for success and being as happy for them when they succeed as when you yourself succeed.

One of the greatest rewards of leadership is the realization that you played a part in helping someone else be successful. Few things are more gratifying than helping someone grow, improve and succeed. A leader's finishing touch with a team should be a mix of appreciation and inspiration. When the answer to the question is found and implemented, everyone wins.

Leadership is much more art than science. It can be learned and absorbed only by doing, starting with mastering yourself. You must lead yourself first; you must be the example and the model for others to see and follow.

CHECK YOUR EGO AT THE DOOR

If you are leading efficiently, you will receive praise. It is OK to accept praise, but never believe it totally. Ancient Romans had a tradition of welcoming home victorious military commanders with a parade that included the leader riding in his chariot. Legend has it that a slave standing next to him would hold a golden laurel above his head and whisper into his ear, "Remember, you are mortal." True or not, it is a good lesson for anyone who achieves success to remind himself that success is earned, not given. You need to keep earning it.

We discussed earlier that leaders have to believe in themselves or no one else will. Your belief in your own leadership abilities has to be strong and durable, but such self-assurance cannot be allowed to become arrogance. So often leaders make poor decisions because it seems their ego is speaking more loudly than their voice of reason. A healthy ego is OK to be a successful leader. Do not let it inflate so that you suddenly have all the answers and it becomes your way or the highway.

It's okay if other people think you're God, but you're in trouble if you start believing it. You can't be a great leader if you make it all about yourself. You must focus on working with your team to accomplish great feats. Egotistical leaders do not care about those around them; they will do whatever it takes to win and make themselves look better. They can be described not as a person who thinks too much of themselves, but as someone who thinks little of others - whether that is breaking rules, cutting corners or making someone else look bad.

Egotistical leaders brag about their own successes instead of celebrating team accomplishments with their teammates. They are only worried about one thing... What makes me look better and what's in it for me? By being an egotistical leader, you lose the team camaraderie and trust. The star of the team is the team. No one person is bigger than the team.

Your team is all on the same bus. Leaders aren't any more special than individual contributors, and everyone is needed to have a successful team. If you view leadership as service, you should consider your team members more important than yourself. Get your ego out of the way and you'll be on your way to success.

ONCE YOU MASTER YOU, IT'S NOT ABOUT YOU

Once you have learned to lead yourself first and are the model to see, you then progress to knowing it's never about you, even though you may be in the spotlight more often than not. During good times, you will get more credit than you deserve. During difficult periods, you will shoulder most of the burden and blame.

Leadership is fighting for hearts and souls of others and getting them to believe in you. Help others get ahead.

Believe in others more than they believe in themselves and you will be more than a leader - you will be a transformer of lives.

We all have platforms we can use to make a difference in the lives of those in our circle of influence. We must give or add value to the lives of those we lead and those around us. You can actually help yourself by helping others. Remember, we always stand taller with someone else on our shoulders.

> "If you want happiness for an hour, take a nap.
> If you want happiness for a day, go fishing.
> If you want happiness for a month, get married.
> If you want happiness for a year, inherit a fortune."
>
> **Chinese proverb**

If you want happiness for a lifetime, help others.
H.O.P.E.

In 1984, Lou Whittaker led a five-man team consisting of American-born men to the peak of Mt. Everest. This was the first all-American-born team to summit the world's largest mountain. Five months into the expedition, the group had reached the final campsite at 27,000 feet. However, Whittaker had a dilemma; all five members were highly motivated to reach the highest peak, but two had to go back to the prior camp for food, water and oxygen.

Once they had the essentials to keep them alive, they returned to the summit they just left earlier that day. After making the grueling mission, they were in no physical or mental state to try to reach the peak. Whittaker would not be one of the team members to summit Everest. When asked why he didn't assign himself the summit run, he answered by saying, "My job was to put the other people on top of the mountain." His answer showed his selfless understanding of his team and the strength of his leadership.

> Whittaker understood when you put the good of others ahead of yourself to achieve a goal, everyone involved wins.

H.O.P.E. stands for Helping Other People Excel, which is exactly what Lou Whittaker was able to do. The more you lose yourself in something bigger than yourself, the more you will gain from the experience.

Inspire to leave a legacy of greatness in that this world was a better place because you were here, not because you are gone. Leave this world a better place than you found it. Stay filled with H.O.P.E. today. Be rewarded with serving others and helping them reach their summit.

LEARN TO LISTEN

In Stephen Covey's book *The 7 Habits of Highly Effective People*, one of the habits he mentions is about being able to understand people by listening to them. The phrase "seek first to understand, then to be understood" is Covey's way of saying it may be in your best interest as a leader to listen to someone first because you may not know how to reach them if you don't. Remember that the people you lead have different ways of being reached effectively. For some, getting in their face and being stern is what works; for others a more sensitive approach is needed and will yield better results. A leader knows what buttons to press because a leader knows the people he or she is leading.

> *"Almost everything in leadership comes back to relationships. The only way you can possibly lead people is to understand people. The best way to do that is to get to know them better."*
>
> **Mike Krzyzewski**
> **Duke Men's Basketball Head Coach**

> *"My biggest criticism of this season is that our coaches didn't invest enough time developing relationships with and really getting to know our players."*
>
> **Nick Saban, Alabama Football Coach**
> **On why his team underachieved in 2013**

LEADERS LISTEN

A great leader listens. I mean really listens. To be able to connect with people's hearts, you must use your ears. You can be the smartest person in the room, but if you can't connect with others, you'll fail as a leader. Leaders encourage their followers to tell them what they need to know, not what they want to hear. You were blessed with two ears, two eyes and only one mouth. That means we were created to listen and watch four times as much as we were intended to talk. You have to be SILENT to LISTEN. Notice that those letters are interchangeable.

S − I − L - E − N − T

L − I − S − T − E − N

ACTIVE LISTENING

Active listening is one of the most important skills for a selfless leader to have. The SOLER method is an easy and effective way to be an active listener.

S – SQUARE UP

Turn to face the person and give them your full attention.

O – OPEN UP

Ask a question that will prompt them to speak and lets them know you are ready to listen. (What's up? What's going on? How's everything going?)

L – LEAN IN

Lean towards them to listen more intently.

E – EYE CONTACT

Be sure to look them in the eye when they are speaking.

R – RESPOND

Give them a meaningful reply after they finish speaking to show them you have really focused on what they were saying. Avoid phrases like *uh-huh, yep,* or *gotcha*.

TALK WITH vs. TALK TO

Coaches would be wise to invest more time "talking with" their players than "talking to" them. Leaders hit a home run when they care enough to listen and think long enough to understand.

People don't care what you know, until they know that you care.

Leadership begins with the heart, not the head. It flourishes with a meaningful relationship, not more regulation. You can love people without leading them, but you cannot lead people without loving them.

People don't always remember what you say, but they will always remember how you made them feel. Choose your words wisely; our words have the power to lift moods and change attitudes.

ROLE ACCEPTANCE VS. ROLE EXECUTION

As leaders, you want to encourage the execution of roles and not role acceptance. Yes, you do want the role to be performed to the best of the person's ability. You don't want people to settle for just accepting their roles. You want them to strive for more and execute their current role on the team to the best of their ability. For a team to be successful, all members should strive to be the best they can be, in the role they were assigned. When all team members strive for personal success and forget about personal achievements, the team will be more productive and successful.

They should always strive to be more. If you want more, you must become more. That is what leaders should convey to their teams. Sometimes people's greatest challenges are coming to grips with their role on the team. Before you can advance to a higher position on a team, you must first be excellent at the role you were assigned. It behooves you to let the people on the bench know that they contribute to the team just as the starters do.

 COACHING POINT: Evaluate your relationships with your closest teammates by answering the questions below.

SELFLESS LEADERSHIP:
TEAMMATE ASSESSMENT

Names:_____

1) What is their favorite sport?

_____

2) What is their favorite kind of music?

_____

3) Who is their role model?

_____

4) What do they like the most about your sport?

_____

5) What do they dislike most about your sport?

_____

6) Who do they trust the most/least on the team?

_____

7) What do they want to do for a living?

_____

8) What one word would they use to describe the team?

_____

9) What one word would they use to describe the coaches?

_____

10) What is their biggest strength?

_____

11) What is their biggest weakness?

_____

Check your answers. Is your relationship as close as you thought?

List the two most selfless persons you know:

_____

What do they do that makes you say they are selfless?

_____

_____

List the two most selfless teammates you have:

_____

What do they do that makes you say they are selfless?

_____

_____

What are some things selfless leaders do in practice?

_____

What are some things selfless leaders do in competition?

_____

What are some things selfless leaders do in school?

_____

What are some things selfless leaders do in the community?

_____

As a leader, what is selflessness to you and how can you demonstrate it to your team?

_____

_____

_____

_____

_____

_____

_____

12:00 SUMMARY

It's about WE, not me.

Check your ego at the door.

Leadership is fighting for hearts and souls of others and getting them to believe in you.

H.O.P.E. – Help Other People Excel.

Leaders listen. To listen, you have to be silent.

You can love people without leading them, but you cannot lead people without loving them.

Focus on role execution instead of role acceptance.

12:00 APPLICATION

What are 5 key points you can apply to yourself and your team from this chapter?

1) _____

2) _____

3) _____

4) _____

5) _____

ABOUT THE AUTHOR

WHO IS BRIAN M. CAIN?

Brian M. Cain, MS, CMAA, is a #1 best-selling author, speaker, trainer and expert in the fields of Mental Conditioning and Peak Performance. He has worked with coaches, athletes and teams at the Olympic level and in the National Football League (NFL), National Basketball Association (NBA), National Hockey League (NHL), Ultimate Fighting Championship (UFC), and Major League Baseball (MLB).

Cain has also worked with programs in some of the top college athletic departments around the country including the University of Alabama, Auburn University, Florida State University, the University of Iowa, the University of Maryland, the University of Mississippi, Mississippi State University, Oregon State University, the University of Southern California, the University of Tennessee, Vanderbilt University, Washington State University, Yale University, Texas A&M, TCU, Baylor, the University of Georgia, the University of Vermont, and many others.

Cain has worked as a mental conditioning consultant with numerous high school, state and national championship programs. He has delivered his award-winning seminars and presentations at coaches' clinics, leadership summits and athletic directors' conventions all over the country. As a high school athletic director, he is one of the youngest ever to receive the Certified Master Athletic Administration Certification from the National Interscholastic Athletic Administrators Association.

A highly sought-after Peak Performance Coach, clinician, and keynote and motivational speaker, Cain delivers his message with passion and enthusiasm, in an engaging style that keeps his audiences energized while being educated. As someone who lives what he teaches, Cain will inspire you and give you the tools necessary to get the most out of your career.

Please visit www.briancain.com/monday to sign up for his weekly newsletter. Also, visit www.briancain.com/calendar to see when Cain will be in your area so you can experience the benefits of having him come in and work with your team.

WHERE'S CAIN?

Cain's Calendar:

"I want to book Cain when he's in town."

ABOUT THE CO-AUTHOR

WHO IS BRETT K. BASHAM?

Brett Basham is a leadership performance trainer with Brian Cain Peak Performance. He is a former All-SEC catcher at the University of Mississippi (Ole Miss) and professional baseball player in the San Diego Padres organization. He was a captain for the 2009 SEC Champion Ole Miss Rebels.

Upon completion of his professional career, Basham turned to the coaching ranks. He began his career at LSU-Eunice in 2012. In his time there, Basham helped lead the Bengals to a NJCAA record 57 wins and only 5 losses on their way to the 2012 NJCAA National Championship.

Basham currently resides in Birmingham, Alabama, with his wife Mary Margaret. He received his Bachelor's Degree from Ole Miss in 2009 and a Master's Degree in Sport Management from The University of Alabama in 2014.

ADDITIONAL RESOURCES

HOW YOU CAN CONTINUE TO BECOME A MASTER OF THE MENTAL GAME

Cain offers a range of training materials to get you and your team to the top of your game. Available at www.BrianCain.com

MASTERS OF THE MENTAL GAME SERIES BOOKS
MENTAL CONDITIONING RESOURCES

Champions Tell All: Cain provides you with all access to some of the World's greatest performers. Learn from mixed martial arts world champions and college All-Americans about mental toughness.	
The Daily Dominator: **Perform Your Best Today. Every Day!** You get 366 Daily Mental Conditioning lessons to help you start your day down the path to excellence. Investing time each day with Cain is your best way to become your best self.	
The Mental Conditioning Manual: **Your Blueprint For Excellence** This is the exact system Cain uses to build champions and masters of the mental game. It has helped produce NCAA and High School champions, MMA world champions, and more.	

So What, Next Pitch!
How To Play Your Best When It Means The Most
A compilation of interviews with top coaches and players where Cain teaches you their systems and tricks. Learn from the insights of these masters of the mental game.

Toilets, Bricks, Fish Hooks and PRIDE:
The Peak Performance Toolbox EXPOSED
Go inside the most successful programs in the country that use Cain's Peak Performance System. Use this book to unlock your potential and learn to play your best when it means the most.

The Peak Performance System (P.R.I.D.E.)
Personal Responsibility In Daily Excellence
This big, video-based training program is Cain's signature training program for coaches, athletes and teams. It will take you step by step to the top of the performance mountain.

Diamond Domination Training:
The New 4RIP3 System for Baseball and Softball
This training program is being used by 11 teams in the NCAA top 25 in college baseball and 8 of the top 25 in college softball. It will help you and your team to unlock your potential and play the best baseball and softball of your life.

4RIP3 MMA Mental Conditioning System
Get the techniques used by the best fighters in the world and start bringing the fighter you are in the gym into the cage. It will help you unlock your potential, teach you drills to sharpen your focus and give you the confidence of a champion.

And more at www.BrianCain.com

CONNECT WITH CAIN

YOUR LINK TO DOING A LITTLE A LOT, NOT A LOT A LITTLE

 www.twitter.com/briancainpeak

 www.facebook.com/briancainpeak

 www.linkedin.com/briancainpeak

 www.youtube.com/wwwbriancaincom

 www.briancain.com/itunes

SIGN UP FOR BRIAN CAIN'S
MONDAY MENTAL CONDITIONING MESSAGE

Cain's Monday Message is full of information to help you unlock your potential and perform at your best when it means the most. Subscribe for FREE and get a bonus audio training. www.BrianCain.com/Monday

CONCENTRATION GRIDS

ONE NUMBER/ONE DAY AT A TIME

 Brian Cain Peak Performance, LLC
Concentration Training Grid
www.BrianCain.com

86	54	04	72	20	05	34	79	52	17
73	43	50	70	44	12	28	59	94	35
45	62	63	97	51	95	91	67	84	75
27	69	23	00	08	83	09	41	65	78
80	39	68	47	29	93	36	30	38	42
61	53	19	48	49	74	40	18	15	21
60	01	14	22	64	07	58	02	32	16
13	31	26	71	66	33	06	85	10	89
76	46	98	37	99	24	57	11	55	82
92	25	81	96	87	88	77	03	56	90

 Brian Cain Peak Performance, LLC
Concentration Training Grid
www.BrianCain.com

86	54	04	72	20	05	34	79	52	17
73	43	50	70	44	12	28	59	94	35
45	62	63	97	51	95	91	67	84	75
27	69	23	00	08	83	09	41	65	78
80	39	68	47	29	93	36	30	38	42
61	53	19	48	49	74	40	18	15	21
60	01	14	22	64	07	58	02	32	16
13	31	26	71	66	33	06	85	10	89
76	46	98	37	99	24	57	11	55	82
92	25	81	96	87	88	77	03	56	90

Brian Cain Peak Performance, LLC
Concentration Training Grid
www.BrianCain.com

86	54	04	72	20	05	34	79	52	17
73	43	50	70	44	12	28	59	94	35
45	62	63	97	51	95	91	67	84	75
27	69	23	00	08	83	09	41	65	78
80	39	68	47	29	93	36	30	38	42
61	53	19	48	49	74	40	18	15	21
60	01	14	22	64	07	58	02	32	16
13	31	26	71	66	33	06	85	10	89
76	46	98	37	99	24	57	11	55	82
92	25	81	96	87	88	77	03	56	90

Brian Cain Peak Performance, LLC
Concentration Training Grid
www.BrianCain.com

86	54	04	72	20	05	34	79	52	17
73	43	50	70	44	12	28	59	94	35
45	62	63	97	51	95	91	67	84	75
27	69	23	00	08	83	09	41	65	78
80	39	68	47	29	93	36	30	38	42
61	53	19	48	49	74	40	18	15	21
60	01	14	22	64	07	58	02	32	16
13	31	26	71	66	33	06	85	10	89
76	46	98	37	99	24	57	11	55	82
92	25	81	96	87	88	77	03	56	90

Brian Cain Peak Performance, LLC
Concentration Training Grid
www.BrianCain.com

86	54	04	72	20	05	34	79	52	17
73	43	50	70	44	12	28	59	94	35
45	62	63	97	51	95	91	67	84	75
27	69	23	00	08	83	09	41	65	78
80	39	68	47	29	93	36	30	38	42
61	53	19	48	49	74	40	18	15	21
60	01	14	22	64	07	58	02	32	16
13	31	26	71	66	33	06	85	10	89
76	46	98	37	99	24	57	11	55	82
92	25	81	96	87	88	77	03	56	90

Brian Cain Peak Performance, LLC
Concentration Training Grid
www.BrianCain.com

86	54	04	72	20	05	34	79	52	17
73	43	50	70	44	12	28	59	94	35
45	62	63	97	51	95	91	67	84	75
27	69	23	00	08	83	09	41	65	78
80	39	68	47	29	93	36	30	38	42
61	53	19	48	49	74	40	18	15	21
60	01	14	22	64	07	58	02	32	16
13	31	26	71	66	33	06	85	10	89
76	46	98	37	99	24	57	11	55	82
92	25	81	96	87	88	77	03	56	90

Brian Cain Peak Performance, LLC
Concentration Training Grid
www.BrianCain.com

86	54	04	72	20	05	34	79	52	17
73	43	50	70	44	12	28	59	94	35
45	62	63	97	51	95	91	67	84	75
27	69	23	00	08	83	09	41	65	78
80	39	68	47	29	93	36	30	38	42
61	53	19	48	49	74	40	18	15	21
60	01	14	22	64	07	58	02	32	16
13	31	26	71	66	33	06	85	10	89
76	46	98	37	99	24	57	11	55	82
92	25	81	96	87	88	77	03	56	90

Brian Cain Peak Performance, LLC
Concentration Training Grid
www.BrianCain.com

86	54	04	72	20	05	34	79	52	17
73	43	50	70	44	12	28	59	94	35
45	62	63	97	51	95	91	67	84	75
27	69	23	00	08	83	09	41	65	78
80	39	68	47	29	93	36	30	38	42
61	53	19	48	49	74	40	18	15	21
60	01	14	22	64	07	58	02	32	16
13	31	26	71	66	33	06	85	10	89
76	46	98	37	99	24	57	11	55	82
92	25	81	96	87	88	77	03	56	90

NOTES PAGES

KEEPING IT ALL IN ONE PLACE

_____

_____

_____

_____

_____

_____

_____

_____

_____

_____

_____

_____

_____

_____

_____

_____

_____

_____

_____

_____

_____

_____

_____

_____

_____

_____

_____

_____

_____

_____

_____

_____

_____

_____

_____

_____

_____

_____

_____

_____

_____

_____

_____

_____

_____

_____

_____

_____

_____

_____

_____

_____

_____

_____

_____

_____

_____

_____

_____

_____

_____

_____

_____

_____

_____

_____

_____

_____

_____

_____

_____

_____

_____

_____

_____

_____

_____

_____

_____

_____

_____

_____

_____

_____

_____

_____

Made in the USA
Charleston, SC
28 April 2015